RAILWAY HERITAGE

DAWN OF THE DIESELS
1959-70
Part 3

RAILWAY HERITAGE

DAWN OF THE DIESELS
1959-70
Part 3

First-generation diesel locomotives and units captured by the camera of

John Spencer Gilks

Edited by Mike Esau

Silver Link Publishing Ltd

First published in 2003

British Library Cataloguing in Publication Data

A catalogue record for this book is available from the British Library.

ISBN 1 85794 173 X

Silver Link Publishing Ltd
The Trundle
Ringstead Road
Great Addington
Kettering
Northants NN14 4BW

Tel/Fax: 01536 330588
email: sales@nostalgiacollection.com
Website: www.nostalgiacollection.com

The number appended to each caption is the negative number. Requests for prints may be made via the Publishers.

Printed and bound in Great Britain

Half title **Greenway Halt (closed 1959), Gloucestershire; GWR railcar, 4.08pm Gloucester-Ledbury, 21 March 1959.**
I always found these railcars stuffy and noisy to ride in but, of course, the Great Western Railway was a pioneer in acquiring and operating them. The Halt is in the sort of location I love – far from anywhere in deep, glorious rural country. Other pictures of the service appear on page 39 of my first book, *Classic Steam: Journeys round Britain*, reprinted as *The Nostalgia of Steam* (Silver Link Publishing, 1994 and 2001). *1537*

Page 2 **Gateshead High Level Bridge, Tyne & Wear; DMU, Sunderland-Newcastle, 30 June 1967.**
Stephenson's bridge was years ahead of its time by combining rail and road in one structure; road traffic was charged a toll collected by North Eastern Railway employees. In this view the route bearing left enters Gateshead Station and continues to Sunderland and along the coast to Hartlepool and beyond. To the right re-enters the East Coast Main Line, providing a second entry into Newcastle Central Station. The Anglo-Scottish Motorail used to run in by the High Level Bridge so that when it reached its destination it had been turned round and the cars were facing the right direction! *C7626*

Title page **Culworth Junction (closed 1966), Northamptonshire; 12.15pm DMU, Nottingham (Victoria)-Marylebone, 5 August 1965.**
This junction was vital in the development of the Great Central Railway in the late 1890s, for the branch to the left led to the Great Western at Banbury and gave access to the South Coast and West of England. Its situation was amid the meadows of Northamptonshire and the OS map was necessary to locate it by car. I have encountered a bull in seeking to reach the signal box and, unusually, have no track permit, so I'm relying on the signalman's kindness and co-operation. He did not fail me and probably thought that if someone was sufficiently keen to find him he must be OK. The DMU to London was followed soon afterwards on to the branch by the Newcastle-Bournemouth, so the complete operation could be photographed within half an hour or so. *C4194*

This page **Stainby Sidings, Lincolnshire; Class 14 with wagons to Market Overton, 28 September 1969.**
I suspect that the Health & Safety Executive would not take kindly to the conveyance of folk in open wagons entered and left by temporary ladders, but to the best of my knowledge of 40 years no one has been hurt. Ironstone was the mineral found in these hills and usually it would gain access to the East Coast Main Line at High Dyke or the Midland at Ashwell and near South Witham. It was lucky that it was a sunny day! *C5399*

Opposite **Northenden Junction, Greater Manchester; Class 25 No D5275, Great Rocks-Winnington freight, 16 September 1967.**
What struck me on my first visit here was the obvious antiquity of the signals, dating back to the days of the Cheshire Lines Committee. Shortly to the west of this scene were two very high posts bearing similarly old co-acting distant signals in both directions almost opposite each other. The line to the Peak from which the train is emerging is now the more important route; no longer can you go ahead to Stockport (Teviot Dale), Woodley and Godley as in the days of the Great Central to Sheffield and beyond. My friend, Dr Ian Cantlon, is busy with his camera too! *C4127*

CONTENTS

INTRODUCTION

This is my third book in the series, and illustrates the early days of diesel traction in the UK, with barely a handful of pictures taken as late as 1970, our deadline. Most date from the 1950s and '60s before the Beeching closures had got under way, and when most trains had more than a couple of coaches.

I recall a young friend of mine contrasting in 1960 the tiny space allowed a passenger in the back seat of a Mini – with his knees nearly on his chest – to that provided to one wise enough to remain with the train. Nowadays times have changed, and often it doesn't do to have long legs in Standard Class; indeed, a sort of claustrophobia can grip a person crammed into a coach with sealed windows and doors when marooned between stations by traction failure or the like. And more time then seems to be spent analysing responsibility for the failure than getting on the move again. Nowadays obtaining a decent meal on board is the exception.

Earlier readers will know that my knowledge of the UK

Above left Guiseley, West Yorkshire; DMU, Bradford (Forster Square)-Ilkley, 7 April 1969.
The reason for this picture is sad. Several stations ahead was a mental hospital, and one of the patients had caused an incident. Our train was therefore held here for some time, hence the opportunity to wander round. Today the line carries frequent electric trains on the overhead system, which facilitate commuting from places like Ilkley and its surroundings into the old West Riding centres of commerce and administration. But incredibly during the Beeching era its future was in doubt and it was kept running entirely at British Rail's own expense in the 1970s without financial help from central or local government sources while local politics were sorted out. C8265

Left Bodiam, East Sussex; John Spencer Gilks, 7 June 1993.
How contented I look on a summer day apparently awaiting a train. But the rails are rusty and I would have been there for seven years before the preserved Kent & East Sussex Railway provided me with a service. In the meantime I was driven to Northiam by Dr Gerry Siviour, my successor at the 'Talking of Trains' class at Surbiton in Surrey (see earlier books), and travelled from there to Tenterden in some style in the 1st Class carriage of a six-wheeled Great Eastern Railway coach looking like Mr Pickwick and feeling very happy. *Dr Gerry Siviour*

railway system is derived in part from circular rail tours, especially on Bank Holiday Mondays, with friends – 'Three Men in a Train', as it were. We were able to take dinner on the express back to London. I have always been more interested in the scene than the train itself. Photographic spots were noted on Ordnance Survey maps and visited later by car with the camera.

In preparing this book I have become very conscious of resurrecting the past: a time when railway stations didn't exist just to provide a platform to assist access to a train, but had buildings, toilets, gardens, signal boxes, character to mirror their communities, and, above all, staff. People who shared the benefits of the railway – and its shortcomings – knew its geography, and could make you feel at home when issuing a ticket or tending a garden, or sending off a train. They would represent the railway in the local business community such as at the Rotary lunch. Now the unstaffed station can be an unfriendly place, especially at night, and a daunting prospect.

We talk of those days as if they were some sort of luxury well beyond our reach in the fourth richest community in the world! A sign bidding us 'Welcome to...' is no substitute, and rightly the subject of a cynical retort. And as for the constantly changing style and remote operation of passenger information screens, I am satisfied from observation that they require maintenance most of the time and probably cost more than the staff they replace.

Recently, while I was at Birmingham (New Street), the 12.18 to Liverpool was announced as cancelled, with profuse apologies. So be it – such events are bound to happen from time to time. But the apologies would have been more acceptable if the speaker had gone on to advise passengers to join instead the Holyhead train at 12.21 and travel to Crewe (perhaps operated by a different company?), where more Liverpool services were likely to be available. Similarly, later that day the 20.45 to Longbridge was said to be 15 minutes late; when the equivalent 20.54 was cancelled, no one pointed out that the late-running previous train had yet to leave!

This is not unique to Birmingham. It is symptomatic of the standard of the railway today, which we have come to accept as the norm, and how sad it is, especially when journeys by road are also becoming so difficult.

How can we have sunk from the quality of 40 years ago as witnessed by this book to the situation today? Obviously there are many causes, and this is not the place for a detailed analysis, although my generation is responsible through our politicians. But one reason that has always fascinated me is the perceived power of the road lobby.

In my professional life with the Local Authority Associations we had come to have regular quarterly meetings with the Chairman and his supporting staff at BR to discuss matters of mutual interest. One day my office phone rang and someone at the headquarters of a leading motoring organisation asked why we were not having similar meetings with them. Having expressed some surprise that they regarded themselves as equals with BR, nevertheless I took myself to their headquarters in 1982 and in a penthouse suite I was regaled with less than flattering spin as to the amount of public money allocated to the trains. An unlikely source of political persuasion, perhaps, and one may wonder how many members knew their subscriptions were put to such a use. Just as little drops of water eventually wear away a stone, so such comments over 40 years and more have led indirectly to Hatfield, Paddington and Potters Bar in more recent times. Concern for the natural environment is used regularly as an excuse for poor maintenance, weeds on the track and journeys through a forest of trees, with the inevitable problem of leaves on the line.

But if we can't turn the clock back in our everyday travels – even I am apprehensive about train journeys today, and not everything was right even then – we can recall what I regard as happier times by means of our archive film.

Some basic facts about the book. The captions to each picture begin with its location (using station names from 1955 and local government areas as in April 1974), then details of the locomotive or multiple unit and its train, and the date on which it was taken, when known; finally there is more detail of the scene and the circumstances in which it was recorded. At the end is the negative number, preceded by a 'C' if it is a colour transparency reproduced in black and white, and 'AL' if the photographer was Alan Lillywhite, one of the 'Three Men in a Train'.

In closing, can I thank, as always, Peter Townsend for the opportunity to use my pictures to entertain other like-minded folk, Mike Esau for putting them together in such a professional way, John Edgington for identifying some of the trains, and Philip Lawson for his editorial assistance. Roger Howard, Don Smith and Reg Williamson have tried to help me become computer literate. The logo was designed by Gavin Mist.

John Gilks
Nawton, 2003

New Holland Pier (closed 1981), Humberside; 1 May 1964.
A journey by car from New Holland in Lincolnshire to Hull in East Yorkshire (both before and after the creation of Humberside) was always interesting. First you acquired your tickets in the barn of a booking hall at New Holland Town Station; then you drove to the point on the platform where the structure narrowed and a traffic light indicated whether you should wait or go ahead to the boat – often a paddle-steamer

– and invariably in my experience retailing stale buns in the cafeteria. The crossing diagonally of the Humber took about 20 minutes unless you were unlucky enough to encounter a sandbank, which fortunately I never did. I often came from my home in Kingston-upon-Thames to Nawton by this route on Friday afternoons before the magnificent Humber Bridge did away with the need for the ferry. This picture of my second (and first new) car long preceded my home in Yorkshire. C6279

1.
SOUTH AND WEST

It was on Thursday 7 July 1960 that I turned my Morris Minor on to the B3212 just west of Exeter and headed for Moretonhampstead. All at once the car slowed down and I found it hard to believe how sluggish it had become. Endless gear changes were necessary and suddenly I realised how steep were the hills of the West Country. This was my first visit by road. Our first railway diversion that day was to Longdown station (closed 1958) at the mouth of a tunnel through which I had passed by train on August Bank Holiday Monday 1956 on the third of the tours I made with Alan and Harry – 'Three Men in a Train' – to cover virtually all of the then British Railways network.

Now I was with Hugh Davies en route to Wenford Bridge to see the Beattie well tanks in action on their long-lived freight workings. The BBC had invited me to record their progress, but due to an administrative oversight they had also asked Peter Semmens to do the same, and we had agreed that he should proceed and I would concentrate on other changes afoot in the region. Hence the tape recorder in the car, interesting events to witness and people to meet, including delivering water churns to Cadhay Crossing near Ottery St Mary on the way home. The same day we discovered a restaurant in Lyme Regis that bore a sign on the door saying 'Closed for lunch'.

On 2 December 1967 one of the societies had been given permission by the Western Region to transfer two locomotives, in steam, from Plymouth to the Bristol area. This was a notable event at the time and I had promised Ian that we would drive down the previous day and trail the locos back as far as Westbury. It so happened subsequently that on the Friday I was invited for interview for the job I was so to cherish later with the Local Authority Associations. Having been offered the job and accepted it, I was asked to see my new boss at 4.00pm that afternoon. How to honour my promise to go to Plymouth? For years it was the talk of the office that their new man's first phone call was to Paddington Station seeking accommodation for the car and sleepers on the night train. This was provided, we woke up in Plymouth, had porridge with Cornish cream at the Continental Hotel, and immediately drove back alongside the engines – in rain, I might add!

It was local government in the form of the Town Clerks of Leicester and Sheffield that persuaded British Rail to make the Western Region transfer to the Midland Region some of its HSTs so that a modern fast service could be provided on the Midland main line as opposed to them ambling round the bends west of Plymouth.

My earliest railway journeys on my own were down the Oxted line when it carried trains not just to East Grinstead and Uckfield but to Brighton, Eastbourne and Tunbridge Wells West. They were very happy days exploring the lovely countryside involved and travelling in trains with antique coaches and locomotives at irregular timings. There are several long tunnels on that line and more than once I have passed through, immersed in steam, in an empty compartment in total darkness or with a glimmer of light from a bulb in a goldfish bowl in the ceiling. The coaches were known as 'birdcage' sets.

You will find that the scene of the first of the photos that follow was reached from Oxted and that we travel around the Southern to end up in the west before transferring to the former Western Region. I hope you enjoy the sensation.

Hellingly (closed 1965), East Sussex; DEMU, Eastbourne-Tonbridge, 23 November 1963.
This station was situated adjacent to a mental hospital, and a siding connected to its private railway system on which vehicles ran by overhead electric traction. Express steam trains for London from Eastbourne came this way to Victoria via Eridge, Edenbridge and Oxted. It was a hilly route with superb views across the countryside. C145

New Romney (closed 1967), Kent; DEMU to Ashford, date unknown.
The condition of the train tells you everything. The green front – yes, before yellow panels were added – is covered with blotches of rust and the whole façade is quite unacceptable. It was not to soldier on for very much longer, although some of these units have survived to run to Uckfield today. The lack of investment is clearly shown in the platform lighting, still by oil lamps in the latter half of the 20th century! C386

Above Doleham Halt, East Sussex; Hastings DEMU, Ashford-Hastings, 8 July 1967.

Every now and again the powers that be announce that electrification (third rail) is shortly to take place between Ashford and Hastings, but invariably it is shelved once more. One of the occasions was when Eurostar arrived at Ashford and in anticipation of something better the aged diesel units extended their run from Hastings to Eastbourne and even to Brighton. Now they are limited to their own bailiwick again. This picture shows one of the main-line units on the Hastings-Tonbridge route, on which some of the tunnels necessitated narrow trains until modern signalling enabled the track to be singled through the various bores. C393

Below Uckfield, East Sussex; DEMU, Victoria-Brighton, 3 February 1966.

The decision to close this line to Lewes, in 1969, was very shortsighted, and news of possible restoration reaches the papers from time to time. The train is approaching a level crossing on what at the time was the A22, a busy main road from London to the coast, and the pundits were anxious to be rid of it and the traffic congestion it sometimes caused. But the station as terminus stayed south of the road, so the crossing remained, and nothing was achieved but the loss of the train service to Brighton. Now there is a bypass to the town and through traffic has ceased here. It's called transport planning! Do notice the gas lamp and Southern Railway notice. The station has moved across the road. C149

TRAIN SERVICES

5o

between **LONDON** *(VICTORIA & LONDON BRIDGE)*
and **OXTED, EDENBRIDGE TOWN,**
EAST GRINSTEAD, TUNBRIDGE WELLS,
UCKFIELD, HEATHFIELD,
BRIGHTON and EASTBOURNE

From 6th JANUARY to 14th JUNE 1964
(or until further notice)

Clapham Junction, Greater London; Charter DMU to Derby via Harrow-on-the-Hill, Clipston & Oxenden and Ashby-de-la-Zouch, 27 September 1969.

This set, exclusive to the Western Region and requiring its own drivers, which I had chartered for the 'Talking of Trains' evening class, was brought here as empty coaching stock (ECS) from Reading. The station announcement of our route and destination was a joy to hear. One of our party insisted on joining at our first stop – Harrow-on-the-Hill – and had to make lengthy explanations to the ticket collector before being admitted to the platform. The next stop was Quainton Road, and soon afterwards we took the Calvert spur and passed above the West Coast Main Line on the Bletchley Flyover. The driver confided in me that he didn't know which would be the authorised route (in practice as opposed to on paper) at Knighton South Junction, Leicester, until the branch signal went off in front of us! C465A

Surbiton, Greater London; Charter 'Blue Pullman' to Carmarthen via Guildford and Reading, 25 April 1970.

Another charter for 'Talking of Trains', and a superior one too. As the journey was about 250 miles each way we thought extra comfort desirable and ordered breakfast and dinner into the bargain. BR charged just £1,000 for all this and for making available another DMU to take us up the Welsh valleys to the various milk depots that were still rail-served – really good value at £8 a head. In order to avoid the fourth rail of the District Line vis-à-vis the ATC used on the WR for safety purposes, the Pullman had to shunt up and down several times at Clapham Junction on its way from Old Oak Common. C543

Above Deepcut, Surrey; DMU, Basingstoke-Woking, 30 July 1966.
While work was in progress to install third-rail electrification to
Bournemouth in the mid-1960s several innovations occurred, and one
of these was the use of Western Region DMUs on local services.
Probably for the first and last time you could see out of the front of the
train and admire Joseph Locke's engineering ability when, in 1839, by
means of deep cuttings complemented by high embankments, he kept
the London & Southampton Railway mainly level for the early steam
engines. C727

Below Wallers Ash, Hampshire; Class 33 and ECS EMU to
Eastleigh, 13 May 1967.
Nowhere was that more true than across the high ground of Hampshire
between Basingstoke and Winchester. Here the double track was later
supplemented by loops for expresses to overtake slower services,
especially freight. One such was at Wallers Ash, where we see empty
stock being delivered in readiness for the electrified service to begin
about a month later. C787

Above **Tisbury, Wiltshire; Class 42 'Warship', Waterloo-Exeter St David's, 26 June 1966.**

While there is modernisation to Bournemouth, retrenchment takes place on the way to the West Country and the Southern route is reduced to a single track west of Wilton so as not to compete with the service from Paddington. To facilitate this it was put under the control of the Western Region (hence 1V74 for a train travelling from the Southern to the Western), which subsequently closed nearly all the network west of Exeter. Already the 'Atlantic Coast Express' had been terminated back at Salisbury. The second line in this picture and the one below is about to be lifted. C1065

Below **Semley (closed 1966), Wiltshire; DMU, Exeter St David's-Salisbury, 26 June 1966.**

In anticipation of rationalisation the sidings at Semley have already been lifted. And it's a Western Region unit that is providing the local service, although it has not called here since March. This station used to be served by a connecting bus to and from Shaftesbury on the hill nearby. C1074

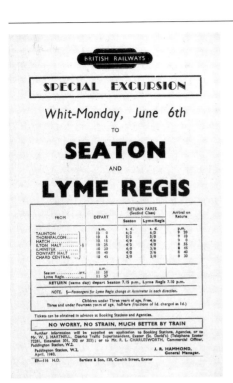

Above Near Combpyne (closed 1965), Dorset; railcar, Lyme Regis-Axminster, 5 March 1964.

It was a charming ride through the hills far away from any significant road, and few could have been the passengers at the wayside halt, but they paid their taxes just like everyone else and had no reduction when they lost their trains. On Summer Saturdays through coaches would come this way from Waterloo, having been detached at Axminster from the main-line train. The viaduct at Cannington suffered a defect and a concrete collar was inserted in one of the arches. The branch had a life of only 62 years. C1126

Below Toller (closed 1975), Dorset; railcar, Maiden Newton-Bridport, 1 September 1964.

A truly rural scene on a line that cut across the grain of the hills well away from any significant road, as was discovered when it became necessary to provide a substitute bus at the time of closure. This did not last long as passengers preferred to use Dorchester and the coast road. Wytherston Bank, between here and Powerstock, proved too much for the 'Bridport Belle' excursion returning from Bridport in January 1967 with nine (rather than the usual eight) corridor coaches, and a diesel engine had to be summoned to assist the two steam engines involved. C1095

Above Chetnole, Dorset; Class 35 'Hymek', Oxford-Weymouth, 3 July 1966.

This line, too, has been reduced to a single track, this time after transfer to the Southern Region, which saw to it that its service from Paddington to Weymouth was cut back and did not compete with its own from Waterloo. Old scores finally settled! This halt survived when others nearby closed. The sun has gone behind a cloud as the train approaches; en route it has come round the Foxhall Junction curve, avoiding Didcot. The Oxford-Bristol service, which has used this in recent years, is about to be withdrawn as I write. *C1082*

Below Grimstone & Frampton (closed 1966), Dorset; DMU, Weymouth-Westbury, date unknown.

Just north of this station stands a very fine three-arch bridge under the line, and it is from this that the road to the station climbs up to the railway. I waited here one sunny Sunday morning – perfect for photography – for a southbound enthusiasts' steam special. Conditions were just right, but after half an hour I had to assume it was not coming – or that I had missed it. Perhaps the mobile phone might be helpful now in such circumstances! *C1107*

Above Weymouth Quay, Dorset; Class 03 with van, 22 September 1962.

It was always fun to travel along the streets from a point adjoining the town station to the quay. On every occasion the men on foot accompanying the train had to move cars parked too close to the track. The boat train for the Channel Islands came this way regularly, returning to Waterloo at 3.45pm. For years a GWR pannier tank headed the procession carrying a bell that was rung constantly to warn others of its approach. I recorded the event for the BBC on 11 July 1960 – what a long time ago! *AL391*

Below Honiton Bank, Devon; Class 42 'Warship', Waterloo-Exeter St David's, 14 August 1966.

My reason for being here that particular day was to see an enthusiasts' special hauled by the locomotive *Blue Peter*, which followed the train in the picture. It was an operating disaster! The 'Pacific' stalled before the top of the bank and had to build up a new head of steam. On the return run by the Western route it proved to be the train for which I waited the longest in my photographic career – more than 3 hours near Frome! Honiton Bank is 1 in 80. *C1135*

Left Copplestone, Devon; Class 35 'Hymek', Ilfracombe-Exeter St David's, 30 June 1966.
Below left Lapford, Devon; DMU, Exeter St David's-Ilfracombe, 2 July 1966.
Above Portsmouth Arms, Devon; Class 35 'Hymek', Exeter St David's-Ilfracombe, 12 June 1970.

I always feel that the country north-west of Crediton is a sort of no-man's-land with this railway trespassing into it. It's now known as the 'Tarka Line' and terminates at Barnstaple, whereas in former days it carried expresses from Waterloo to Ilfracombe and to Torrington. Because of its isolation I am including three pictures of it. Portsmouth Arms is of special interest as the landowning family here also had an estate near Hurstbourne – a closed station between Basingstoke and Andover – and could travel from one to the other by direct line. *C1167/C1170/C1174*

Below North Tawton (closed 1972), Devon; DMU, Plymouth-Exeter St David's, 30 June 1966.

If you study the picture you can see just how straight – and how hilly! – the Southern main line to Plymouth was hereabouts, a real racetrack. After closure a single line was retained to gain access to the ballast available for track maintenance from Meldon Quarry, and it is still used from time to time by passenger trains to the preserved station at Okehampton. *C1212*

Near Meldon Junction, Devon; railcar, Exeter St David's–Padstow, 2 July 1966.
The lonely railcar heads into even lonelier country west of Dartmoor. All the branches in this part of North Devon and Cornwall were closed because of lack of passengers outside the tourist season, and as so few people live here that can be no surprise. I've often thought that Beeching would have us all huddled into towns, and only then could we have a train. Most domestic budgets rely on smoothing out income and expenditure over a number of items; however, each branch line had to stand on its own feet and pay its way. In sparsely populated areas this was impossible. It's even lonelier here now! *C1221*

Above **Halwill Junction (closed 1966), Devon; DMU, Bude-Exeter St David's, 2 July 1966.**

The line from Halwill to Torrington was difficult to use within a day from my home at Kingston-upon-Thames. We managed it once, however, by using the sleeper from Paddington to Exeter and taking the first local train on the Southern to the northern end. The chairs on the sleepers at Watergate Halt were dated the year the line opened – no financial loss there. *C1226*

Below **Whitstone & Bridgerule (closed 1966), Devon; DMU, Bude-Exeter St David's, 1 July 1966.**

The station name always reminds me of a science laboratory! The station was about 2 miles from each of the villages it was provided to serve. Now it is nearly 40 miles to the nearest railhead. *C1231*

Camelford (closed 1966), Cornwall; railcar, Padstow-Exeter St David's, 1 July 1966.
Readers with a keen eye will notice that I took the car on a tour of this area in early July 1966. I was sorry not to have come earlier to see the through steam trains to London. By the time I arrived the Western Region had taken over, and all was gloom and doom. I recall waiting at Tresmeer station one evening. There wasn't a sound. The passing loop had gone and the signal box, the well-tended garden was full of weeds, and the station building was totally neglected. Above all there were no staff to look after you. The railcar came and went. There were no longer any passengers. Now this situation applies to urban stations as well. *C1242*

Padstow (closed 1966), Cornwall; railcar to Exeter St David's, 29 August 1966.
This was one of John Betjeman's favourite places and he is buried nearby. The line followed the River Camel from Wadebridge and passed over a creek by a large metal viaduct as it approached the terminus. We were on one of our railtours, having left Plymouth at 9.00am for Liskeard. From there at 9.35 we went to Looe, returning again by the 10.10am. The 10.48 took us to Bodmin Road and the 11.35 to Padstow. We started for home at 12.45, pausing for lunch in Wadebridge. On again at 2.25 to Halwill and at 3.58 to Okehampton – no fear of missed connections. The 4.38 took us to Exeter and the 5.58 express back to Surbiton (at 9.49pm) with an excellent dinner on the way. *C1249*

Above Tavistock North (closed 1968), Devon; Class 42 'Warship',
Brighton-Plymouth (1V65), 1 July 1966.
Just look at the spectacular surroundings, the station being sited high
above the town to help the line keep a reasonable incline by Dartmoor.
It became 'North' as a result of nationalisation, to identify itself from
'South' in the valley below on the Great Western route from
Launceston to Plymouth. This was the only decent train left, as the
London service had been truncated at Exeter and DMUs operated
westwards until closure. 3609

Below Turnchapel (closed 1951), Devon; Charter DMU from
Yealmpton, 11 April 1959.
I described this charter by the Railway Enthusiasts' Club in the first
volume (page 11), with the argument about using a DMU and further
illustrations in the second (page 6), so I will add no more. 1572

Above left **Wargrave, Berkshire; railcar, Henley-Twyford, 31 December 1960.**

Now we come to the Great Western proper and transfer our allegiance from the Southern Region. Travelling from Henley, until recent years it was nearly always necessary to change trains at Twyford on the main line, but improvements have been made and some now run through, after reversal, to Reading, and there is still one peak-hour train to and from Paddington. There is a public footpath to reach the viaduct over the Thames, but to discourage access a 'Private' sign was close to each edge of the path when I used it last. *C1570*

Left **Southcote Junction, Berkshire; DMU, Paddington-Newbury, 12 October 1964.**

I had to obtain a track permit to wander on the line at this junction, which otherwise is difficult to photograph. My main purpose was to record the Newcastle-Bournemouth express while it was still steam-hauled, and having done so I then hung about to take a few other shots including the one you see. Just look at all the telephone wires and the height of the telegraph poles. *C1646*

Above **Upton & Blewbury (closed 1962), Berkshire; Railcar, Didcot-Newbury, 31 March 1962.**

What wonderful lighting in this picture! I was driving back from Cricklade and the state of the sky led me to divert to this station and wait to picture the train. I was not disappointed. Those readers with an eagle eye will notice that the same day I had been at Yeoveney Halt on the outward run. *2610*

Above left Newbury, Berkshire; ex-GWR railcar to Didcot (and 'Hall' No 5947), Bristol-Devizes-Paddington.
A picture by Alan, the second of the 'Three Men in a Train' on our mammoth railtour of the UK. Newbury had a bay at each end of the up platform, that to the south being occupied by the service to Lambourn until 1960. The railcar is destined to go through Upton & Blewbury on the other track. *AL26*

Left Near Radstock, Somerset; Class 35 'Hymek', freight to Bristol via Pensford.
Note the former Somerset & Dorset Railway route at the top of the picture running parallel into separate stations in Radstock. The line on which the freight is running was unusual in being closed, then re-opened. I had planned a charter in the area in 1968 and was advised officially of the re-opening in advance; we therefore operated that way, which gave us time to get to Cheddar later – real initiative and co-operation from the Western Region. I have included a handbill (*right*) from 1959 for an excursion from stations on the branch to Barry Island. *C1735*

Above Witham (closed 1966), Somerset; DMU, Weymouth-Bristol (and steam-hauled local to Yatton), 11 May 1963.
The sort of country junction I enjoy visiting – approached only by country lanes and a few miles from the nearest main road. Its main purpose was to act as an exchange platform between the West of England main line – although only the Bristol-Weymouth service normally called – and trains to Shepton Mallet, Wells and ultimately Yatton on the Bristol & Exeter route. It's surprising that the station lasted for three years after the branch service was withdrawn. It remains a very important junction for aggregate traffic from the nearby Mendip quarries to road and rail building schemes in London and elsewhere. *C1739*

PLEASE RETAIN THIS HANDBILL FOR REFERENCE

WESTERN **BRITISH RAILWAYS** REGION

Special Excursion

SUNDAY, JUNE 21st

TO

NEWPORT, CARDIFF

AND

BARRY ISLAND

| FROM | DEPART | RETURN FARES SECOND CLASS ONLY | | | ARRIVAL ON RETURN |
		To Newport	To Cardiff	To Barry Island	
	a.m.	s. d.	s. d.	s. d.	p.m.
FROME	9 30	8/9	10/3	11/9	10 20
MELLS ROAD	9 40	7/6	9/0	10/0	10 10
RADSTOCK WEST	9 50	7/3	8/9	9/9	10 0
MIDSOMER NORTON & W.	9 55	7/0	8/6	9/6	9 55
FARRINGTON GURNEY‡	10 0	6/9	8/3	9/3	9 50
HALLATROW	10 5	6/6	8/0	9/0	9 45
CLUTTON	10 10	6/3	7/9	8/9	9 40
PENSFORD	10 20	6/0	7/6	8/6	9 30
BRISLINGTON	10 30	5/9	6/9	7/9	9 15
ARRIVAL TIMES		a.m. 11 40	p.m. 12 5	p.m. 12 30	

Return train will leave Barry Island at 7.20 p.m., Cardiff (General) 7.50 p.m., Newport (High Street) 8.10 p.m. the same day.

‡—Tickets to be obtained from the Agent: Mr. C. Kingman, "Miners' Arms", Farrington Gurney, before date of travel.

Children under Three years of age, Free; Three and under Fourteen years of age, Half-fare.

NOTICE AS TO CONDITIONS.—These tickets are issued subject to the British Transport Commission's published Regulations and Conditions applicable to British Railways exhibited at their Stations or obtainable free of charge at station booking offices.

Tickets can be obtained in advance at Booking Stations and Agencies.

Further information will be supplied on application to Stations, Agencies or to Mr. H. BASTIN, District Commercial Manager, Transom House, Victoria St., Bristol 1 (Telephone 2-1001, Extension 211 or 212); or to Mr. A. E. FLAXMAN, Commercial Officer, Paddington Station, London, W.2.

Paddington Station, W.2, May, 1959.

J. R. HAMMOND General Manager

Printed by J. W. Arrowsmith Ltd., Bristol (87/388) H.D.

Venn Cross (closed 1966), Devon; DMU, Taunton-Barnstaple, 2 July 1966.
The signalman has come out of his box to exchange tokens with the driver so that the single line concerned can remain safe. Do notice the gibbet-style gantry by the tunnel entrance, which enables the driver to see the signal as he enters the far end. DMUs did not run for very long on this line, replacing on Saturdays through steam services from Wales and the Midlands to Ilfracombe. C1787

Liskeard, Cornwall; DMU to Looe, 29 August 1966.
Here the branch platform is at right angles to the up platform on the main line, although there is a connection on the north-eastern side. The train will turn full circle to the south and pass under the main line before completing a sort of horseshoe into Coombe, then reversing to Looe. A freight train follows the same route from time to time, but instead of reversal it goes ahead to a quarry. The branch is an interesting survivor, due in part to inadequate parallel roads so that a substitute bus service is virtually impossible. C1901

2.
WALES AND THE MARCHES

The first time I took bed and breakfast for myself was in the village of All Stretton, south of Shrewsbury, in Shropshire, at the gateway to the Marches in July 1956. I had been on a weekend course on railways at Attingham Hall with Charles Clinker, the great historian, and Charles Hadfield, of canal fame, and this had been a new experience for me. Mr Clinker had rightly criticised my first article in *The Railway Magazine* (August 1955) in a letter the following month, so I went to the course to learn how to do better. I had hired a car for ten days in order to explore the area now under review.

The course finished on Sunday afternoon and I looked for accommodation, which I found at White Hart Cottage with a Mr and Mrs Hall. They could not have been kinder. In those days en suite facilities were rare, and Mrs Hall left a jug of hot water with a washing bowl outside the bedroom door for me to use. On the first day I explored remnants of the Bishop's Castle Railway (page 32) and reached the town I have since visited probably more than anywhere else; there is a shop there now that sells second-hand LPs, the ingredients of my other hobby. My diary tells me I had a picnic lunch at Stanner Halt (closed 1951) between Kington and New Radnor. By way of some small return for her kindness I took Mrs Hall to Devil's Bridge and we travelled on the narrow gauge to and from Aberystwyth, a pleasure you can still experience today.

I have described in earlier books where my abiding interest in railways came from. It had been markedly stimulated in Wales in August 1953 when Hugh Davies made arrangements for three of us to journey there. On Monday the 17th we turned up at Abbey Foregate station in Shrewsbury to be the guests of the Army on a Wickham Railcar over the Shropshire & Montgomeryshire Railway to Llanymynech. That evening we alighted from the connection at Abermule and made our way to a Youth Hostel, which I was dreading! I am a dreadful snob! We cadged a lift for part of the walk from the station and I shall never forget opening the door of the converted school,

seeing all the exhausted, red-kneed people there, and bidding them 'good evening' with absolutely no response. My duty proved to be to make porridge in the morning. I had persuaded Hugh to ring for a taxi (then against YHA rules, I believe) and we were soon on our way to the 9.22am train to Aberystwyth. After a trip on the Vale of Rheidol we reached Mrs Jones of 11 Cambrian Terrace, Towyn, at 7.45pm. The Talyllyn Railway, newly restored to use, was visited, and at 7.26am on the Thursday we left for Moat Lane Junction (closed 1962). Although trains still pass the site, no longer can you change there for Brecon via Builth Wells, Three Cocks Junction and Talyllyn Junction. It was a superb ride, much of it hard by the River Wye, and on every occasion I had marvellous weather; I miss that line more than any other. We changed into the train to Newport, which provided a real contrast in scenery. First through the Brecon Beacons, where a narrow gauge line has now been put in place from Torpantau, the summit – really magnificent country – but then emerging from a tunnel into Pant station and to Dowlais Top station, a real shock at the appalling ugliness of the heads of the South Wales Valleys from which coal and other minerals were then extracted. I was glad to get home.

On the first day of February 1962 Bob Kirkland and I joined the 1.00pm coal train from Penallta Colliery near Ystrad Mynach to Cadoxton near Barry Docks, which passed over Taff Vale on the Walnut Tree Viaduct. We asked the driver if he would be good enough to stop thereon for photographs. He agreed, provided his locomotive was on terra firma on the far side, so we were held in the brake-van in the middle of outer space. It was bitterly cold and windy – my cap blew away, never to be seen by me again – but the photos were acceptable, even though dark shadows persisted at that time of the year. We moved on along the former Barry Railway to Tyn-y-caeau Junction, with that company's line from Pontypridd and the spur to the South Wales Main Line at St Fagans, used by the 5.35pm from Cardiff to Pontypridd until 1962. The junction signal box was to be burned down by vandals, resulting in closure of this great Welsh railway and its replacement in part by a motorway. We went on through Wenvoe Tunnel to our destination. A really memorable journey. We begin our journey in the Marches and end up in North Wales.

Above left **Severn Tunnel, Caldicot, Gwent; Class 47 Paddington-Swansea (1F65), 31 July 1965.**
And so we enter Wales. Above the cutting on the right can be seen another double-arm signal guarding the junction on the older line from Gloucester via Chepstow, which has a smart halt at this point. Trains still follow the older route from Swindon via Stroud when engineering work requires the tunnel to be closed. Until 1960 trains from Bristol in those circumstances could use the Severn railway bridge at Sharpness. C2972

Left **Near Mathry Road, Dyfed; Class 52 'Western', Paddington-Fishguard (1F16), 23 May 1970.**
The line from Clarbeston Road to Fishguard fascinates me. It wasn't built until 1906 to coincide with the development of the port and its shipping service to Rosslare in Eire, and finds its way through a deep gorge of the Western Cleddau River near Treffgarne. This is preceded by a tunnel from which the line emerges on the hillside so high above an intersecting lane that itself passes through a tunnel, which is constantly illuminated. Until 1964 there was a service of steam auto-trains from Clarbeston Road – now a small community of that name – calling at a variety of halts. Then boat trains were all that remained, one running from Paddington to be in Fishguard at lunchtime and

another in the early hours of the morning, supplemented for a short time by a daytime Motorail service from Olympia. Gradually these have been withdrawn, the winter service operating only from Swansea and the line reduced to a single track. In 2003 no through London trains were likely to run. Photographic locations of interest are difficult to come by, but the farmer at Tre-coed has been good to me more than once, allowing me to wander across his farm. On my first visit – to record Letterston Junction from on high – he bade me hurry as men were currently knocking down the signal box there. The shutter clicked and immediately afterwards the roof of the box was lifted off! C3223

Above **Dorrington (closed 1958), Salop; Class 47, southbound coal train (8Z84), 28 March 1970.**
We're in the Marches now along the Welsh border, with Offa's Dyke not so far away. Until quite recent years this north-south route carried through trains from Liverpool and Manchester to the West of England, but it was reduced in status and these became restricted to Summer Saturdays. Today the service – albeit far more frequent – normally links Manchester with Cardiff, although there is a train this way to Penzance again and another to Waterloo via Salisbury. Freight links Shotton on Deeside with South Wales steel works. C2837

Stretford Bridge Junction (closed 1935), Salop: Class 47, Manchester-West of England, 17 July 1965.
This was the point – note the depression in the ground on the left – at which the Bishop's Castle Railway set out for Montgomery but ended up at Lydham Heath, with a branch to the country town. Edwards Griffith records in his little book on its history that he could look out of the carriage window, observe the track sink below the locomotive and rise behind the last coach with a dash of surface water going into the air. Unless reconstruction has taken place recently the bridge from which this picture is taken has low iron railings like a bed-end, and the car can be parked thereon until the train appears. C2875

Rye, East Sussex; DEMU, Ashford-Hastings, 8 November 1969. I'm with friends from Tonbridge and we have come here because the line is threatened with closure – but it survives, as recorded earlier (page 11). Do notice that the signal box is remote from the level crossing; accordingly there have to be two people employed as the crossing is opened by hand, even in wet weather. I imagine this may have been remedied by now with modern telecommunications advising the signalman that replacement barriers are down –but this may not have happened! 389

Above Yeoveney (closed 1962), Surrey; railcar, West Drayton-Staines West, 31 March 1962.

This rural scene existed within 17 miles of central London until 1962. Now it is under or adjacent to the M25 and peace reigns no longer. As a boy it was the railway part of a circular tour I used to make from Kingston by bus via Hounslow. In those days the service was operated by auto-train with pannier tank, and I think we were pushed towards Staines, but memory may play tricks. I'm sure it contributed to my subsequent lifelong enjoyment of railways. The halt was reached across a field and gave no protection from the weather. *1512*

Below Thrupp, Gloucestershire; Class 35 'Hymek', Gloucester Central-Swindon (2B29), 17 October 1964.

This was a superb autumn day with brilliant sunshine. In addition there seemed to be a never-ending stream of goods trains up Sapperton Bank towards Swindon. Coupled with the Chalford steam auto-train going up and down the Golden Valley, what more could one desire? Fortunately, in retrospect, the through local train was diesel-hauled, so can appear in this book. *2126*

Above Blockley (closed 1966), Gloucestershire; Class 35 'Hymek', Worcester (Shrub Hill)-Paddington (1B68), 14 September 1963.

Over the Cotswolds and a few miles to the north-east of Thrupp runs the former Oxford, Worcester & Wolverhampton Railway, now largely reduced to a single track but still carrying expresses between Paddington and Hereford and sometimes weekend diversions from far and near. On this day I left home in the car at 6.40am through autumn mist – so my diary records - and eventually arrived at Verney Junction so timed as to pick up Harry and Alan on arrival of the train from Banbury –the other two of the 'Three Men in a Train' – and carried them home to Guildford. Extraordinary! *2469*

Below Williton, Somerset; Class 35 'Hymek', Minehead-Paddington (1A28), 13 June 1970.

One of the later pictures in this book, and before closure and re-opening by the preservation society, who have done so well here. Dr Cantlon and I had to make a judgement: if we saw this train, could we then drive at a reasonable speed across Exmoor through Simonsbath to arrive at Mortehoe station on the Ilfracombe line in time to see the train from Paddington? The answer proved to be 'yes', but it had already passed the station when we arrived and we had to picture it across a rather anonymous field instead. *1779*

Above left Hersham, Surrey; Class 42 'Warship', 11.00am Waterloo-Salisbury, 1 January 1965.

What a disgrace! This is the famous 11.00am from Waterloo, the 'Atlantic Coast Express', until the Western Region put its malign influence on it and cut back its destination to Salisbury. However, the 10.54 Waterloo-Basingstoke local still got out of its way at Hampton Court Junction, and has just come through on the slow line behind a 'West Country' 'Pacific'. So all is not lost. 583

Left Micheldever, Hampshire; Class 47, up 'Bournemouth Belle', 13 May 1967.

The station here is almost the last between Waterloo and Southampton at which you can alight in open countryside, Winchfield being the other. And now it is threatened with a New Town to make up the numbers of houses expected to be needed by those who wish to live in the South East. I'm glad I'm in North Yorkshire, even if Fylingdales is just down the road. The station was originally known in 1840 as Andover Road, quite a walk without a horse. Do notice that the 'Bournemouth Belle' is in decline – the red van hardly matches the colour of the Pullmans as in days of yore. Electrification is barely a month away. 786

Above Halterworth Crossing, Hampshire; DMU, Romsey-Eastleigh, 1 April 1967.

This line has had a chequered history in recent years, and the principal station – Chandler's Ford (pictured in my earlier *Nostalgia of Steam* volume, page 14) – has been closed since 1969. The Solent Plan evidently expects it to be rebuilt and a new service introduced, at least between Romsey and Eastleigh, but the Strategic Rail Regulator has his eye on it in the current round of reductions. The crossing, signal box and signal are of London & South Western Railway origin; today there is just an automatic lifting barrier here. 979

Above **Ropley, Hampshire; DMU, Eastleigh-Alton, 5 July 1969.**
I just had to include this picture, for the grass on the left is now the workshops and yard of the Mid Hants Railway – the 'Watercress Line' – where it rebuilds and houses its preserved locomotives. When I was involved professionally with the local authority in trying to stave off closure we could not understand how the service could lose money. After closure we discovered that it hadn't and that a pig-headed man at BR HQ was at the root of the problem (see T. R. Gourvish, *British Railways 1948-73*, page 449). *711*

Below **Sparkford (closed 1966), Somerset; DMU, Weymouth-Bristol, 3 July 1966.**
Just look at the lovely flowers in the station garden – someone obviously loves and tends it. The station closed the following October and the formation is now a single track, but at least the trains still pass through. *1079*

Yeovil Junction, Somerset; Railbus, Yeovil Town-Yeovil Junction, 3 July 1966.
Look at the vast area covered by this junction built by the Southern Railway but adjacent to the former Great Western Castle Cary-Dorchester route and connected to it in the early days on the right of the picture and again further north during the Second World War (pictured in *The Nostalgia of Steam*, page 162). The railbus looks quite lost. Don't miss the gantry of upper quadrant signals at the end of the up platform. *1110*

Above left Okehampton, Devon; Class 42 'Warship', Brighton-Plymouth (1V65), 1 July 1966.
Here is the Brighton-Plymouth train again, this time in colour, and it is passing the loading dock formerly used by the Motorail service to Surbiton, which was introduced to avoid the gridlock that occurred each summer on the Exeter Bypass. That itself is now bypassed by the M5, but still congestion occurs in the peak of the holiday season. Obviously the Western Region is busy dismantling the bay so that it cannot compete with its train to Newton Abbot (see page XI). *1217*

Left Lydford (closed 1968), Devon; DMU, Plymouth-Exeter St David's, 2 July 1966.
An interesting picture: on the right is the former GWR route from Launceston to Plymouth with its characteristic signals, and the Second World War connection from the Southern main line put there in anticipation of possible diversions. In happier times it was used by the REC special pictured above (page 23). Do notice Brent Tor on the horizon. *1256*

Above Launceston (closed 1966), Cornwall; railcar, Exeter St David's-Padstow, 30 June 1966.
Both the Great Western and the Southern built independent stations at Launceston, but the former (on the left) was closed in 1952, although retained, as its signal bears witness, for freight until the grand finale. *1236*

Egloskerry (closed 1966), Cornwall; railcar, Padstow-Exeter St David's, 30 June 1966. A tall telegraph pole, wires, a lamp post and cast iron trespass sign all combine to give this picture an old-fashioned look. It has only another three months to survive, and probably no oil lamp will ever be put in the globe again. 1238

Above Bodmin Road, Cornwall; railcar, 11.35am to Wadebridge, 29
August 1966.

A wet Bank Holiday, yet there is quite a crowd for the train, some
having come direct from Plymouth. The sign still proudly says change
for Bodmin, Wadebridge and Padstow, but only for another four
months, although the Bodmin & Wenford Railway has since re-
opened part of the line. The station is now called Bodmin Parkway.
1245

Below Exeter St Thomas, Devon; Class 52 'Western', Olympia-
Newton Abbot Motorail (1C35), 30 June 1966.

This fine Brunelian station has since lost its overall roof but is retained
for local people to get to Sainsbury's. For the return journey in 1969,
the cost of a driver, a car under 14 feet long and up to three passengers
was £25 each 2nd Class and £29 1st Class with reserved seats. The
equivalent cost today (to Penzance) is not stated in Table 501 of the
national timetable, but credit cards are accepted. *1828*

Below Pen-y-Groes (closed 1964), Gwynedd; DMU, Portmadoc-Bangor, 22 May 1962.
The closure of the line between Afon Wen and Bangor (and between Carmarthen and Aberystwyth) deprived the Welsh of a through line from south to north within the Principality, and in my judgement encouraged their nationalism – a train via Ludlow is no substitute. Two stations south of here – Brynkir – is where the main road turns east across the hills to Portmadoc while the railway goes south-west down the valley and along the coast. One day we took the train but came back by the short-cut road on the bus. The timing of bus and train at Brynkir were very tight (and not intentional, I suspect), so we visited the station man there a day or two before and arranged for him to hold the train if necessary. It wasn't in the event, but it guaranteed our dinner that night. *3581*

Right Ffestiniog Tunnel (north end), Gwynedd; DMU, Llandudno-Blaenau Ffestiniog, 31 May 1970.
What a superb view! This picture appeared in black and white in the first volume in this series, but we thought it deserved a re-run now that colour is available. You are looking across the vale to the east Snowdon range. *3683*

Above West Mill (closed 1964), Hertfordshire; DMU, St Margarets-Buntingford, 4 July 1964.

Back to the outer London area now, and to a line that closed despite its potential for house values and to stockbroker commuters to the City. Most trains necessitated a change at the junction with the line from Hertford East. It has another three months to run and retained its rural atmosphere to the end. Steam trains had not long ceased to operate from their shed at Buntingford. I am driving to photograph trains at Newport (Essex), Bartlow, Fulbourne (strangely no negative in the collection), Lord's Bridge, St Neots, Potton and Sandy. 5559

Below Althorne, Essex; DMU, Southminster-Wickford, 12 October 1963.

The commuters did benefit here, with electrification and through trains sometimes to Liverpool Street, not only at peak hours. Property values will have been enhanced by this capital investment in the railway. I haven't been there for years, but no doubt nature still provides the interesting autumn mists arising from the nearby River Crouch, with its sailing potential. 5623

Above **Dullingham, Cambridgeshire; DMU, Ipswich-Cambridge, August 1969.**
Passengers are waiting to be taken to Cambridge or beyond. The station survived, whereas nearby Six Mile Bottom and Fulbourne succumbed, but the formation has been reduced to a single track. 5683

Below **Dunham (closed 1968), Norfolk; DMU, King's Lynn-Norwich, 11 May 1968.**
The epitome of the rural branch-line station: presumably the buildings have been sold off, even though this meant that passengers had to cross the track to reach the train. In my opinion there was no excuse for withdrawing a train service connecting such thriving communities as Norwich and King's Lynn, with Wymondham, Dereham and Swaffham en route. It must have been possible to make it pay. Presumably 10 per cent of the Eastern Region network had to be shut under Beeching/Margetts come what may. The western extremity of the line from Middleton Towers has been retained for a weekday train of industrial sand to West Yorkshire. 5854

Middle Drove (closed 1968), Norfolk; Class 31, King's Lynn-March parcels, 11 May 1968. More than 4 miles west of the King's Lynn-Ely line (at Magdalen Road station, now renamed Watlington), and more than 5 miles east of Wisbech, this station was sited nowhere in the Marshland Fen and was approached by very narrow lanes. What a joy to visit! Because the new DMUs lacked adequate storage space, initially special parcels trains ran to make up the deficit, then such traffic was discouraged and discontinued. 5946

Above Easton Court (closed 1961), Hereford & Worcester; former GWR railcar W23, 12.10pm Woofferton-Bewdley, 22 October 1960.

At this charming backwater west of Tenbury Wells I have taken advantage of a public footpath to cross the line. I'm spending the weekend at The Howard Arms, Ditton Priors, and exploring the countryside around. We even went to Craven Arms after dinner on the Friday evening to watch the mail train pass through on its way south. *2292*

Below Montgomery (closed 1965), Powys; DMU, Aberystwyth-Shrewsbury, 3 September 1966.

The town of Montgomery, with its square off the main street and imposing Town Hall at the west end, looks the prototype for election night when the result of the poll was announced from its balcony and drinks were on the house all round! The station was some distance away and passengers tended to head to and from Welshpool. This is reaffirmed by an excursion from there to the Blackpool Illuminations on Sunday 6 September 1959 (see the handbill reproduced below). Passengers left Welshpool at 11.25am and, hopefully, alighted at 2.36am on Monday morning in time to go and do the milking. *C3441*

Tal-y-Cafn & Eglwys-Bach, Gwynedd; DMU, Llandudno-Blaenau Ffestiniog, 31 August 1968.
What a tongue-twister, but what a tourist trail along the Conway Valley and up through the mountains. Over the years track capacity has been reduced, but it has survived and connects with the Ffestiniog down to Portmadoc. Recent experiments suggest that heavy freight trains may return to bring out slate dust; the nuclear flasks no longer run to Trawsfynydd Power Station, which is being decommissioned. C3663

Above Llanderfel (closed 1964), Gwynedd; DMU, return Barmouth-Blythe Bridge excursion, 23 August 1959.

The contrast with today's railway portrayed by this picture could not be greater. Who today would bring out signalmen and open 54 miles of track exclusively for one return train on a Sunday evening. I had no foreknowledge of this and could not believe a youngster over dinner in the nearby hotel who told his mother a train was coming. I left my soup to hurry out with the camera, but had no time to get on the right side for the sun. *1808*

Below Holywell Junction, Clwyd; DMU, Chester-Llandudno, 3 June 1965.

Today Class 47 locomotives haul Mk 2 coaches through this station alongside some new rolling-stock, which has proved unreliable. I wonder what the Chester & Holyhead Company would have thought of such a situation. Their tariffs were inscribed in slate on the station walls until removal to the National Railway Museum in York. *C3752*

3.
MIDLANDS AND NORTH

My first visit to the North was as a national serviceman in the RAF, and I was obliged to take the train from Euston to Warrington, then, in a cobbled street, join a bus to Padgate to be fitted out in my uniform and learn the rules of the regime. Within a week I was marching across Manchester from Central station to London Road en route for Wilmslow and the square-bashing camp nearby, where I was incarcerated for about six weeks with only one weekend to go free. I was impressed by the line of the Pennines as seen from the parade ground and was determined to explore these in later years.

I returned north next in more agreeable circumstances on an Ian Allan Special on 26 April 1958. It was called 'The Pennine Pullman' and left King's Cross at 9.15am. Between 12.58pm and 1. 12pm it was scheduled to travel from Castleford to Garforth via Allerton Main in order to avoid reversal in Leeds, and must have looked a fine sight crossing the viaduct over the River Calder. We stopped at

Diggle for 5 minutes to have a brief look at the portals of Standedge Tunnel when all four tracks were in use. Both lunch and dinner cost 11s 7d, and a bottle of Medoc was 13 shillings. The menu said that 'it will be appreciated if passengers will kindly bring any difficulty or lack of attention to the notice of the Conductor in charge at the time of service'.

My residence in the North began at weekends in 1974 and involved the use of the 'Cleveland Executive' from King's Cross on Friday evenings with dinner on board, and the sleeper from Leeds overnight on Sunday. I well recall an occasion when the down train approached Challoner's Whin Junction at York some 15 minutes early. There was a buzz of happy conversation in anticipation of the weekend and people were donning their coats when the train stopped and, after an interval, the guard announced that we would be detained here for perhaps 2 hours as a goods train was on fire in Dringhouses Yard just around the corner. But, he said, the driver was a reasonable man

Hayfield (closed 1970), Derbyshire; DMU from Manchester (Piccadilly), 1 October 1961.
Why this short branch was closed is a mystery to me. The trains ran to Manchester, which was a useful lifeline to this community for commuting, shopping and entertainment purposes. The signal box here could have been shut down and the branch run as a single line from the junction at New Mills Central. As it was, that junction and a short section of track in tunnel was retained to enable the Eastern Region stopping service from Sheffield to shunt out of the way of the main-line service then provided by the Midland Region before retracing its steps. *AL1064*

and he and his mate would put down steps at the front of the HST and assist passengers to alight at their own risk. We were adjacent to the main road into the city and could climb up the embankment, scale the railings at the top and thumb a lift into town. I shall never forget the sight of nearly a trainload of passengers doing just that. What would the Health & Safety Executive say today? Now we would be locked into the train with sealed windows and doors and be liable to suffocate. Is that really safer?

Ian Allan Ltd had run the 'High Peak Express' on Sunday 25 September 1955 and this had several unusual features. The main line was taken from St Pancras to Derby, but then most passengers were set down at Whatstandwell station south of Matlock (and still open). Here special buses, which proved to be Midland Red single-deckers with cutaway cabs, were available, and for a fare of sixpence they would take you to Cromford Wharf. I was amazed that we left the station approach fast on a bad sightline and were set down on a blind bend on the A6. Then began the long climb on foot up the incline to Sheep Pasture Top and, if I remember right, up to Middleton Top. Here open wagons were provided for the journey to Friden over the Cromford & High Peak. Because of the steep Hopton Incline two locos were attached and the train was divided into two sets of trucks. We set off on the first sortie and soon realised that we were approaching a narrow tunnel at high speed. The drivers must have thought this a great joke, for as we entered everyone was getting down in the wagons and covering their face and hair to avoid the smuts; I can still feel them today. In the truck ahead of me was a lady in a full-length white coat. We blasted up the bank, then set back into a siding while the locos retraced their steps and brought up the second lot amidst the smoke that hadn't cleared from the first run. All future trips over the line were made from north to south! We deserved the leg of lamb on the way home – no wine listed this time.

That train ran in and out of Buxton via Miller's Dale. For some reason Beeching regarded the Peak route as a duplicate, and hence it was closed in 1967; there is serious talk of re-opening. Buxton might also have lost its service from Stockport, had not a barrister from Mitre Court Chambers in the Strand forced British Rail to release the figures on which it based its case and ridiculed them. As a result even double track survives and an hourly service throughout the day with trains going on to places like Blackpool.

One of my favourite journeys years ago was on the evening train from Blackpool to Preston, Blackburn, Accrington and Burnley, which we usually left at Halifax. It was invariably a Metro-Cammell unit, which seemed to race along with the sun behind us lighting up the Pennines ahead. It seemed to crash over the many junctions with those of us sitting in the front rocking about. There are many short tunnels on the route and we seemed to rush in and out of these without a care in the world. There were few passengers because they would be taken by excursion. This journey can still be made, but it is a wonder for there was a time when the service was curtailed between Burnley and Hebden Bridge; indeed, for a while it was completely withdrawn. At one time there was but one train a day each way and I wanted to use it from Rose Grove (at 2.44pm) to Leeds. It was a professional visit to the Town Hall, and when lunch began I explained to the Mayor that I would like to leave promptly at half past two. This was OK and he said I would be taken to the station. Imagine my surprise, therefore, when I emerged to find a double-decker bus awaiting my pleasure (Burnley-Pendle was municipally operated), and we were at the station in no time. I asked the driver to wait while I made sure that the train was signalled, then went down the steps to the platform. First Class travel was the norm, so I made my way to the front of the DMU. After a quarter of an hour no one had sought my fare, so I went back to find the guard. There were about 20 people on board. He informed me that he was not responsible for ticketing and I should pay at the barrier. It so happened that the unit terminated in a bay close to the ticket collector at Leeds and I asked him how much I owed. No other passenger went that way. It was obvious that he had never heard of Rose Grove and consulted his orange booklet in vain. Did it matter, I asked, that Rose Grove was in the Midland Region? There was so much embarrassment that in the end I gave him 50p and called it a day. That's how lines then lost money and could be closed, especially if a regional boundary was crossed.

I was once asked at my evening class – 'Talking of Trains' – at Surbiton whether there was any reason why we should not hire a coach and take railway photographs as a group, as I did with my car. The key to success would be a driver who entered into the spirit of the occasion, and luckily we found one right away. The first journey took us to Ockendon and Blake Hall in Essex, then round north of London to the Midland main line at Sharnbrook. We continued to the A5 near Weedon in Northamptonshire, and walked about half a mile down a track, which then crossed the West Coast Main Line adjacent to the M1. Looking at those photos now one is struck by the lack of road traffic. Later that afternoon we visited Aynho Junction and ended up crossing a field to a footbridge over the Western main line to Birmingham near Brill. Goodness knows what the local farmer thought of this crowd on his land, however much they had a right to be there. At that time there was but a single track, and the only decent train of the day was the 5.42pm from Paddington, which was loco-hauled. This came past to time, 30 camera shutters clicked, the driver sounded his horn in surprise at seeing so many at this lonely spot, and we all went home – with fish and chips in Thame. It was to be the first of many such outings in the Midlands and the North, where I finally took up permanent residence in 1983.

Above Neston, Merseyside; DMU, Wrexham (Central)-New Brighton, 29 April 1967.
Do notice the Great Central Railway signal still in use on this Cheshire branch, even though it is now on a concrete post. In the distance stands the Shotton Steel Works at Dee Marsh, to which steel coil is brought regularly from South Wales over the southern part of the line. Mrs Barbara Castle, later Lady Castle but then Secretary of State for Transport, took more than two years to reject Beeching's recommendation for closure of this line. The trains were terminated, however, at Bidston rather than New Brighton. *C2828*

Below Helsby, Cheshire; DMU to Hooton.
This junction station is still in full use with services to Warrington and Chester as well as Ellesmere Port. The signal box stands in the apex of the platforms and it is possible to pass the time of day with an agreeable signalman and learn the whereabouts of one's train. *C4072*

Above right South Harrow Tunnel, Greater London; Class 42 'Warship', Birmingham (New Street)-Marylebone, 4 November 1967.
This section of line is pure Great Central and the tunnel is crossed at the far end by the Piccadilly Line of London's Underground when above ground. It was then very rare for ex-Birmingham trains to come this way, but Paddington was closed for engineering work. Now Chiltern Trains run a frequent service from Marylebone to Birmingham (Snow Hill) this way. *C4137*

Right Ashby Magna, Leicestershire; DMU, 12.15pm Nottingham (Victoria)-Marylebone, 26 October 1963.
I have always assumed that it was intended for the M1 to be built on the route of the Great Central at this point but that objections to the closure, which delayed it until 1966, meant that the construction work pictured here had to get under way just east of the original alignment. As a result a bridge had to be provided under the line further north, which is a godsend to those major contractors who are seriously considering the reconstruction of the line from south Leicester to a point from which trains could gain access to the Channel Tunnel. *C4220*

Below Shirebrook South (closed 1931), Nottinghamshire; Class 31 No D5817, 10.31am from Skegness (1E98), 11 August 1962.

A fascinating picture: a regular scheduled Summer Saturday train drawing into a station that had been closed for more than 30 years. The buildings had been levelled, and just before the train appeared a ticket collector arrived on a bicycle and locked the only gate that was an official exit. He then inspected the ticket of every holidaymaker returning from the coast. They must have thought, why did we come home? He eyed my car with suspicion, assuming that I had come to help someone make a quick getaway without paying. This area was a maze of railways prior to nationalisation, and Shirebrook boasted two stations in addition to this one on the Leen Valley line. I have often wondered whether there was an official or unofficial agreement between the National Union of Mineworkers and the National Union of Railwaymen whereby these holiday trains continued running over routes that had no other passenger service. Shirebrook – hitherto Shirebrook West – has returned to the current National Timetable with the restoration of the Nottingham/Worksop service. *2732*

Bottom Torside, Cheshire; Class 37, Manchester (Piccadilly)-Harwich (1E78), 16 May 1966.

I have always thought that the closure of the Woodhead route, however justified by falling coal traffic at the time, was a short-sighted disaster. The line had the misfortune to inherit an outdated DC electrification system whose installation had begun before the Second World War, and it was said that there was no economic justification in going over to today's AC system. Yet the tunnel at Woodhead was not brought into use until 1954, and all traffic ceased between Hadfield and Penistone on 20 July 1981. We often hear Beeching criticised for negative thinking; it is only fair therefore to recall his second report on The Development of the Trunk Routes, which compared parallel routes and came to the conclusion that the Woodhead should be developed between Sheffield and Manchester, and the Hope Valley closed. Indeed, a British Transport film in which the narrator remarks 'some hope for that' was withdrawn from circulation. In the event influential residents of the Hope Valley who worked in Sheffield feared for the loss of a train that they used on snowy days, and such pressure was brought to bear that it survived with its local stations, and Woodhead was doomed. Local public opposition was impossible. The Tintwhistle Rural District, which then absorbed the western half of the Pennine section, had few inhabitants; its revenue came from water supplies. *3571*

Above Verney Junction (closed 1968); Buckinghamshire; railcar, Bletchley-Buckingham, 14 April 1962.

This was possibly my favourite station, in a rural part of North Bucks; because of its isolation from any community it was named after the local landowner. The railways to Banbury and Oxford parted company there from the 1850s, but the station didn't exist until the Aylesbury & Buckingham arrived. Subsequently it became part of the Metropolitan Railway, and in its heyday Pullman trains terminated here from Liverpool Street. It often won the best kept station garden award. Today there is just a single line here deep in undergrowth running from Claydon to Bletchley, but perhaps it will return to use one day when the Strategic Rail Authority has the resources. *2613*

Below Marsh Gibbon & Poundon (closed 1968), Buckinghamshire; DMU, Bletchley-Oxford, 14 May 1961.

I can no longer recall why on this Sunday morning I left home at 6.00am and saw Stanier and Fairburn 4MT Class 2-6-4T No 42090 near Finmere on the first train of the day from Woodford Halse to Marylebone. All I do know is that I then went on to take this picture, and I'm glad I did so. Do notice the oil lamp – a new train amidst ancient facilities. *C3806*

Above Theddingworth (closed 1966), Leicestershire; DMU, Ely-Birmingham (New Street), 26 October 1963.
Another sparkling new train set running through a station with a disused goods yard and signalled by a London & North Western Railway lower quadrant. The timetable here had received such scant attention over the years that trains still called at some of the wayside stations only on market days lost in the mists of obscurity. *3025*

Below Madeley Junction, Telford, Salop; DMU, Wellington-Leamington, 10 March 1963.
It would be hard to find a location so changed by the years. I went there again last autumn and the junction is now surrounded by the office buildings of Telford New Town, and the signal box has been moved across the tracks to the apex of the branch, presumably to facilitate exchange of tokens with the coal trains that pass that way to Ironbridge Power Station. The parapet of the bridge has been raised considerably, and I could only take the new picture by standing on tiptoe. *2837*

Honeybourne West Loop, Hereford & Worcester; Class 47, diverted Midland express (1B19), 15 August 1970.

The Great Western did not build its line from Stratford-upon-Avon to Cheltenham until the early part of the 20th century, and because it ran parallel to the older Midland route British Rail decided to downgrade it, then shut it completely. But before they did so, engineering work had to be carried out on the 'competitive' line, and expresses were diverted this way at weekends. The train is northbound and the signal is set for the spur westwards to the Oxford-Worcester line. Because there is no similar connection at Norton, the train would have passed above the Midland there, then through Worcester (Shrub Hill) and Droitwich and rejoined its normal route at Stoke Works Junction near the foot of the Lickey Incline. The Gloucestershire Warwickshire Railway preservation group has re-opened the route between Winchcombe and Cheltenham Racecourse. C2547

Ashchurch, Gloucestershire; Class 47, down express (1V32), 18 July 1965.

I'm driving home from Church Stretton, but the evening light is so magnificent that I break my journey here. The original station is still in evidence, with the platform shaped to take rails to Tewkesbury and Malvern (withdrawn 1961 and 1952 respectively), and on the other side of the train can be seen the siding that is all that remains of the alternative loop to Barnt Green via Evesham. The signal box has been swept away but a new anti-vandal-type station has arisen, served by trains between Nottingham and Cardiff. C2586

Above **Upper Broughton (closed 1948), Nottinghamshire; Class 45, Nottingham (Midland)-St Pancras (1C25), 7 April 1963.**

If you stood on this bridge today you might be surprised by the speed of a Pendolino or some other new vehicle on what is now the Old Dalby test track. The station was closed so long ago that BR's policy of demolition had yet to take effect, so the buildings at street (or lane) level remain untouched – you feel that you might still enter and demand a ticket to London. In fact, the line to the north runs out near Plumtree and the bridge over the Trent now takes road traffic. C4929

Below **Cromford, Derbyshire; Class 45, Manchester Central-Nottingham (Midland) (1D92), 24 February 1967.**

Although no longer part of the Midland route from London to Manchester via Bakewell, this line survives as a single track between Ambergate and Matlock and might see re-instatement beyond. Enthusiasts have already started, and the Peak District National Park Authority is really interested. Not only could it emulate the North Yorkshire Moors Railway, but a through service might be resurrected. I never understood how Beeching claimed this to be a parallel route through the Pennines; Sheffield-Manchester and West Riding-Manchester perhaps duplicate, but this runs from south-east to north-west and the Dore curve is hardly competitive. Do notice the distinctive railway buildings. A leaflet setting out the station closures from 6 March 1967 is reproduced opposite. C5055

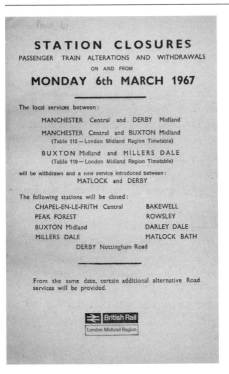

STATION CLOSURES
PASSENGER TRAIN ALTERATIONS AND WITHDRAWALS
ON AND FROM
MONDAY 6th MARCH 1967

The local services between:

MANCHESTER Central and DERBY Midland

MANCHESTER Central and BUXTON Midland
(Table 115 — London Midland Region Timetable)

BUXTON Midland and MILLERS DALE
(Table 119 — London Midland Region Timetable)

will be withdrawn and a new service introduced between:
MATLOCK and DERBY

The following stations will be closed:

CHAPEL-EN-LE-FRITH Central	BAKEWELL
PEAK FOREST	ROWSLEY
BUXTON Midland	DARLEY DALE
MILLERS DALE	MATLOCK BATH
DERBY Nottingham Road	

From the same date, certain additional alternative Road services will be provided.

British Rail
London Midland Region

Above Darley Dale, Derbyshire; Class 25, Manchester Central-Derby (2P53), 24 February 1967.
The enthusiasts have already got here. I'm going to stay in Buxton and drive to the Churnet Valley the next day and Pipe Gate on the Sunday. C5058

Below Bamford, Derbyshire; Class 31 No D5846, Sheffield-Manchester Central (2M85), 11 July 1964.
As we saw earlier (under Torside, page 40) this station was saved primarily for Sheffield commuters. But it is a blessing for the hundreds of ramblers that come out of the cities into the High Peak for fresh air and recreation. At this stage the old world survives with gas lamps and traditional buildings. I've taken my nephew with me to encourage him to take an interest in railways, but his patience is fast running out as he learns that we must await the steam-hauled Llandudno-Sheffield, which proves to be more than 90 minutes late. C5166

Above Cowburn Tunnel, Derbyshire; Class 45, eastbound coal empties, 16 May 1966.

The Hope Valley line enters from the east through Totley Tunnel and exits by the one in the picture. The scenery is superb, yet I have no views from the hills above; I shall have to hurry as age may discourage the climb involved. There are plenty of trains to see on their way between such places as Liverpool and Norwich. C5196

Below Strines, Derbyshire; DMU, Hayfield-Manchester (Piccadilly), 4 January 1968.

The trains calling here today tend to unite Sheffield and Manchester. It was the 'right kind of snow' on the day of my visit; I've driven from Stafford and am going on to Stretton near Warrington. This was near the end of the steam era and visits to this hotel – with convenient access to the M6 for northbound sorties to Lancashire – were quite frequent. C5097

Above Bollington (closed 1970), Cheshire; DMU, Macclesfield-Manchester (Piccadilly), 13 September 1969.

This was a relatively little known line built by the North Staffordshire Railway jointly with the Great Central. It is now a stub end at Rose Hill, Marple, with a service to Manchester (Piccadilly) worked by the oldest DMUs in town. Presumably the journey is so short that it doesn't matter that much if they break down. I once transferred from this line at Higher Poynton station to the LNWR station at Poynton by walking a mile or so. 3669

Below Lostock Junction, Greater Manchester; DMU Manchester (Victoria)-Blackpool North, 19 July 1968.

This is the point at which trains for Wigan and Southport diverge from those to Chorley and Preston, and only the latter now make calls here. The land on the left has been turned into a neat car park, and I sometimes eat my lunchtime sandwiches there when travelling out from Nawton. On the occasion of the picture I am again based at Stretton. C9204

Below Ravensthorpe (Thornhill LNW Junction), West Yorkshire; DMU, Leeds-Manchester (Victoria), 22 July 1967.
The track layout has been revised since this picture was taken in order to enable faster running to and from Leeds, which has by far the greater number of passenger trains. The four-track section from Wakefield (ahead) has been reduced, and today there are just three lines between here and Mirfield, one of which is bi-directional in operation. The station has been modernised. *C4611*

Bottom Diggle Junction, Greater Manchester; DMU, Leeds-Manchester (Victoria), 9 July 1966.
This junction, too, has been remodelled. The lines on the right used to provide an alternative route to Stalybridge, but have been lifted and accordingly the crossover no longer exists. Diggle is at the southern end of Standedge Tunnel, under the Pennines that crown the picture, and the first place in what used to be Lancashire. The only level stretch of track is in the tunnel and used to be the site of water troughs between the tracks where locomotives took supplies on the move – what a mess there must have been! *C4664*

Right Saddleworth Viaduct, Greater Manchester; DMU, Manchester (Victoria)-Leeds, 22 July 1967.
While waiting to take this picture I could hear movement on the cliff-face on which I was standing and suddenly a climber hove into view complete with grappling irons. Below the cliff face in front of me ran the branch to Delph, closed to passengers in 1955 (to goods in 1963). I recall a memorable photo by Eric Oldham hereabouts. *C4673*

Below right New Hey, Greater Manchester; DMU, Manchester (Victoria)-Rochdale, 9 July 1966.
What a spectacular site for a church! Today the sidings have gone and only a single line remains to Rochdale. I believe that this branch – like the one from Bury – is to become a tramway into Manchester. For this visit Ian and I were based in Holmfirth, famed since for *Last of the Summer Wine*. The lady who gave us B&B was renowned justly for her food, although to park there I had to go forward into a church lychgate, then back across the road, and find a sticky car in the morning from the lime tree overhead. *C4673*

Above Ewood, Lancashire; Class 25, Blackburn-Bolton vans, 19 July 1968.

Here come the vans, probably operated for the reasons given under Middle Drove above. In the background Blackburn is being turned into a town of high-rise flats, which to me seems totally out of character. As a result today the journey by car from Darwen to the north seems endless. C8347

Below Walton's Siding, near Blackburn, Lancashire; DMU, Blackburn-Manchester (Victoria), 14 April 1967.

The railway climbs out of the Ribble Valley at Blackburn through Darwen, then through a long tunnel before spreading out at this point – or at least it used to. Now just a single line survives, carrying trains from Clitheroe to Manchester. During the reconstruction of the West Coast Main Line some expresses are likely to come this way to reach the Settle & Carlisle, as they have done in the past. C8344

Above Nappa, North Yorkshire; Class 47 No D1806, up parcels (3K17), 25 June 1967.

Such trains will eventually arrive here. This section of track between Clitheroe and Hellifield sees very few regular trains, but the one in the picture used to come along at around 10 o'clock every Sunday morning and disturb the rust on the rails. The metal bridges under the line where it crosses the A682 have never seen a lick of paint in the 40 years I have been visiting the area. C8392

Below Wennington, Lancashire; DMU, Morecambe-Leeds, 30 September 1967.

This used to be an important junction, and in steam days trains from Leeds were regularly divided here, the main portion going ahead to Lancaster (Green Ayre) and Morecambe and the remainder to Carnforth. Later a stop was provided on eastbound steam excursions for a run-past here. When the direct route through Halton was closed in 1966 the surviving service was extended from Carnforth along the WCML to Lancaster, reversing there before going on to the coast. At Carnforth there used to be a spur enabling through running from Wennington to, say, Grange-over-Sands, and when I was Secretary of the Friends of the National Railway Museum I chartered several trains over it, including one with *Mallard* on which duck was served at dinner. Now the line has been lifted. Happily double track survives from Settle Junction to Carnforth, but normally it is a single signalling section of 26 miles or so, and takes about 40 minutes to clear; there are signals at Wennington, but I haven't seen them at stop for years. C8597

Above **Lunds, North Yorkshire; Class 25 No D5188, freight to Carlisle (5M31), 24 June 1967.**
This was a day on the Settle & Carlisle based at a favourite farm by the line at Giggleswick, where the peace is now ruined by the adjacent bypass. In earlier days I was able to stick a microphone on the end of a boom out of the bedroom window and catch the sound of a steam train leaving Giggleswick station and climbing up the bank; by thus using a Ferrograph tape recorder connected to the mains, no hum occurred.

Those tapes are still in my collection and I enjoy them, even though they are mono. What a mixture of vehicles this freight is conveying – a real train! AG C8954

Below **New Biggin (closed 1970), Cumbria; Class 45, down 'Thames-Clyde Express', 4 September 1965.**
When the Settle & Carlisle was saved from closure this station did not re-open, even though sited right within the village. I wonder why? *3525*

Above **Helm, Cumbria; Class 47 No D1620, up express (1M46), 11 August 1968.**
We're waiting for the return of the 'Fifteen Guinea' double-headed steam special from Carlisle to Manchester and the weather looks set fair. Through the hill behind runs Helm Tunnel, which is difficult of access for photography. A friend agreed to fly us over there from Teesside Airport in a Cessna in the 1980s, and we managed to picture a steam special emerging southbound before fog came down and aborted the outing. C9018

Below **Baron Wood, Cumbria; Class 45, down 'Thames-Clyde Express', 5 September 1968.**
This picture brings back many memories. Baron Wood was always out of bounds, with numerous warning notices about the outcome of trespass. On this day I thought I would risk it, but as is always my luck I could hear a Landrover approaching as soon as I came near the line. Well, at least I could open the gate and save the driver having to alight, I thought. On being spotted, the driver, who proved to be the landowner, was totally relaxed and said that I should go further up the line where he had had some trees felled to improve the view. He went on to direct me also to this site a mile or so further north where he said the drivers sometimes stopped their trains to collect pheasants from his gamekeeper, a notice to this effect having been posted 3 miles towards Settle. The trespass notices were a legal requirement to overcome some tax problem. I don't know who owns the estate today. C9129

Above Garstang & Catterall (closed 1969), Lancashire; Class 47, up Freightliner (5T47), 29 July 1967.

The line by the outer edge of the down platform used to form the branch to Knott End (closed to passengers in 1930 and to goods in 1950), across the Wyre estuary opposite Fleetwood. The M6 motorway now runs behind the station building. C9288

Below Carnforth (down main line), Cumbria; two DMUs, to Carlisle and (rear) 3.35pm to Windermere, 28 September 1967.

Unusual this, in my experience – the London train diverged here for Barrow in Furness, and two DMUs waited one behind the other to make connections northwards on the West Coast Main Line. Two old-fashioned blackboards indicate their destinations long before electronics could mislead us. Despite the clarity of the situation I still heard some woman ask mistakenly for her train. C9288

Above right Lune Gorge, Cumbria; Class 47, Bathgate-Cowley car carrier, 24 June 1967.

There is a tiny lane winding along the fellside from Sedbergh to Tebay, which I'm told brings back memories of cross-country running to the public school boys there. Despite the mist it is a happier occasion for me, because I'm enjoying a picnic lunch and watching trains on the West Coast Main Line prior to the construction of the M6 above the tracks and an end to the tranquillity. Look at all those vehicles on the carriers, which doubtless will soon fill the motorways. C9356

Right Shap Summit, Cumbria; Class 24, down express, 24 June 1967.

Hardly anyone will need an introduction to this scene, so I will leave it at that. We've come here from Sedbergh. C9405

Above Troutbeck (closed 1972),Cumbria; DMU, Workington-Penrith, September 1964.

By the time this picture was taken the line on which the train is approaching was restricted to the lightweight DMUs, the Summer Saturday steam trains running both ways on the other line from Threlkeld to Penruddock. For some reason my diary is silent about the visit, so the date is taken from the transparency. Nearer Keswick is a lovely British Transport Film location once used to herald *The Six Five Special* on the box. C9425

Below Silecroft, Cumbria; DMU, Carlisle-Barrow in Furness, 25 May 1968.

Do notice the grass on the platforms, which have since been cut back for public use by a barrier. I just love this area and go back there as often as possible from a base at Cartmel, which involves quite an exciting drive over the hills. This is a remote area, which is why, I presume, it is home to the Atomic Energy Establishment at Sellafield and the firing range at Eskmeals. During the 2001 foot and mouth epidemic I decided to picture the nuclear flask train going south in a cutting near Drigg. I therefore parked on wasteland near the bridge, observing that a new barrier had been installed nearby, presumably to deter terrorists. After I had taken the picture a young policeman appeared and asked me if I was all right as he had seen me wandering around as if in a daze. He was exceedingly polite and pleasant and I reassured him before proceeding on my way. I must be getting old! I hastened to the Bower House Inn where my enquiry about the possibility of a full lunch was greeted with absolute delight. Do sit down, she said, you're the first customer this week. C9574

Kent's Bank, Cumbria; DMU, Preston-Barrow in Furness, 18 May 1967.
The Furness Railway built some delightful stations, and this one has survived. The outlook across Morecambe Bay is splendid, and I generally bide awhile here. I'm with the then Chief Structural Engineer of Surrey County Council, and his wife is gracing the seat, which has squirrels cast into the supporting ironwork. It is a rendezvous for those who venture on foot from Arnside into the waters of the bay and walk back here, with experienced guides, I must add. On one occasion last year so many turned up that they were unable to board the railcar that operated that morning and had to wait an hour for the next train. C9475

Above **Whitehaven (Bransty), Cumbria; DMUs to Carlisle, September 1969.**
This station has since been completely rebuilt and is very smart. Corkickle Tunnel behind the left-hand DMU was barred to the sleeper train that used to come nightly from Euston, and it had to terminate at the other end of town, returning ECS to Barrow for the return journey. The tunnel was under repair for years. C9654

Below **Kirkandrews (closed 1964), Cumbria; Class 26 No D5310, Silloth-Carlisle, 6 September 1964.**
The town of Silloth is trying to make a comeback. Its cobbled streets have been retained, and the gardens running down to the Solway where it meets the sea. A regular market is being created. But sadly no trains. Again this is a favourite area of mine and there is a myriad of charming lanes between here and the Maryport & Carlisle line. C9708

4.
THE EAST

I do not like driving in cities. By living in Kingston-upon-Thames I had little choice other than to drive through London if I wished to visit Essex and Suffolk, so such occasions became quite an event and were given much thought as to the route with the least traffic. Now that I live in North Yorkshire the approach to East Anglia is a joy, involving as it does a ride over the Humber Bridge and across the Lincolnshire Wolds.

My first relevant pictures were taken in 1958. By that date the time-honoured railway journeys had revealed potential photographic spots to be visited by car, and I began on the Stour Valley and Colne Valley lines, which was timely because the locomotives and rolling-stock were well past their 'sell-by date' and had to be replaced or the lines closed down. In the event the train services survived for another nine years. These pictures were of steam trains.

Due to the age of existing motive power and coaches, the dawn of the diesels was early in East Anglia and they were employed on many routes that have since been lost. It cannot be said that new traffic was not sought; the pity is that someone somewhere insisted on a set percentage of closure and would not tolerate dissent. Gerard Fiennes, General Manager of the Eastern Region at the relevant time, fought back. He actually went round his bailiwick on a regular basis to see what was really going on. His famous book about trying to run a railway led to his dismissal, but also to the sacking of his boss, the Chairman of British Rail, so he was obviously on to something. His memorial is the East Suffolk Line from Ipswich to Lowestoft, on which he pioneered innovations that saved money and kept the service running. Recently through trains to and from London have been re-instated. One of the problems of maintaining the service is the number of level crossings, and I was instrumental in bringing this to the attention of the National Association of Parish Councils in the vain hope of closing a few of them where alternatives were nearby.

My period of national service was spent mainly at Honington on the Suffolk/Norfolk border, along which ran the 'border line' connecting Bury St Edmunds with Thetford, closed to passengers in 1953. The year before I visited this on a bicycle – Seven Hills Halt was the nearest point to the RAF camp – and made one return journey on the afternoon train. I have the photographic results on 127 black and white film, and Barnham station has been published.

Ely North Junction is crucial to the network, as here the line from London divides into three, to Peterborough, King's Lynn and Norwich, and to avoid a river bridge there is also a loop from east to north-west. The Potter Group has a rail/road business nearby. But how to photograph this so as to illustrate the layout? This problem led to my first pictures from the air. We flew from Biggin Hill in a light Cessna with four seats and went round and round over the site until satisfied that all angles had been covered. What the signalman thought I cannot imagine, and I suspect that today we might be regarded as potential terrorists. Most of the results are satisfactory. We then took in the almost redundant Whitemoor Marshalling Yard, the layout at Lincoln and the railway level crossing at Newark before descending to the airfield near Radcliffe on Trent. I went on to Nawton, while Gavin stayed airborne to record Princes Risborough, another site difficult to photograph in complete form on the ground.

I didn't discover the joys of the Midland & Great Northern Joint Line until almost too late; it closed in 1959. With the exception of an Ian Allan Special DMU, all the trains were steam-hauled, so cannot be illustrated in this book. I have reason to mention it because the A17 from Sutterton to King's Lynn is an unavoidable part of my journey to the east. There are more lorries on that road in an almost continuous stream both ways than anywhere else I know. The irony is that long sections of the road are now based on the former railway track. If that traffic has developed to the extent that it has, how come the railway authorities could not have harnessed it in the past? I believe that this is yet another instance, like the Western taking over the Southern west of Exeter, where old rivalries still existed in the 1960s, for which nationalisation provided long-awaited opportunities to get even! It sounds ridiculous, but I have lived long enough now and witnessed events that tell me I am not far wrong. So the M&GN – a major trunk route – was closed, and branch lines like those to Wells-next-the-Sea, which intersected it at Fakenham, were retained with almost inevitable closure at a later date, so that all was lost. To quote Gerard Fiennes again if I may; he said that when he

became GM he was determined not to put right what needed doing when he was a junior clerk, unlike some of his colleagues.

After the picture of Hunstanton (page 74) our survey of the East moves towards the ECML, then heads north, ending at the Royal Border Bridge. On the way we take in all those branches that used to serve North Lincolnshire, now devoid of lines between Skegness and Cleethorpes and inland. We then cross the Humber and move up the coast, which gradually encroaches on the wolds and moors to Teesside.

Battlesbridge, Essex; DMU, Southminster-Wickford, 12 October 1963.
Today this line carries AC overhead electric trains to Liverpool Street, but at the time of this picture its future was very much in doubt. I felt that I had to come before it was too late, and made one of my rare journeys by car across London using the Rotherhithe Tunnel outward and the Woolwich Ferry when homeward bound. I got as far north as Long Melford in my quest for pictures. *3018*

Cressing, Essex; DMU, Witham-Braintree, 12 October 1963. On the way I called here, another line to be electrified as it happened, which enhanced land values, encouraged commuting to London and creating 'Essex Man'. The folk of Braintree were determined not to lose their railway under Beeching and fought back consistently. By so doing their wishes were granted and enhanced, although westwards to Bishops Stortford disappeared. 3022

Colne Valley Viaduct, Essex; DMU, Colchester-Sudbury, March 1969.
The people of Sudbury had to put up an even bigger fight for their line because it crossed from Essex into Suffolk, and that authority had little interest in London commuting. The land forming the goods yard at Bures was sold off by the BR Property Board for fashionable housing, but the resulting revenue was in a separate account from train operating and did not directly benefit the branch. No doubt the maintenance costs of this viaduct influenced thinking about the future. C5604

Sudbury, Suffolk; DMU to Mark's Tey, March 1969.
Presumably the compromise must have been the closure of the lines to
Bury St Edmunds (from Long Melford) and to Cambridge. Few of the
trains run through to Colchester, and thus involve that annoying
change and wait at Mark's Tey on the main line from Liverpool Street
to Ipswich and Norwich. I came this way for the first time during
national service and recall how fascinating and how antiquated were
the train sets and engines. The terminus has now been resited. A leaflet
recalling the days of through trains is reproduced here. C5595

Manningtree, Essex; Class 47 No D 1771, Liverpool Street-Norwich (1G26), 25 August 1966.

A day's leave from the office and a run round on the trains: 9.30am Liverpool Street-Ipswich; 10.50 to Saxmundham; 11.38 to Aldeburgh and 12.20pm back to Ipswich; 1.19 to Manningtree and 1.47 to Harwich Town. Hence the next picture there, and this one on our return awaiting the 3.40 to Colchester. We ended up by taking the 4.30 to Cambridge via Sudbury and returning to London on the 6.40 from Cambridge to Liverpool Street. Just look at the flowers in the station garden – real PR! C5649

Harwich Town, Essex; DMU, 3.03pm to Manningtree, 25 August 1966.
I haven't been beyond Parkeston Quay since I took this picture so I have no idea whether the station remains untouched.
It was certainly in good shape then. C5660

Melton (closed 1955), Suffolk; Class 37, Liverpool Street-Lowestoft, 13 July 1963.
As you will see I spent this day driving up and down the East Suffolk Line photographing the Summer Saturday extras to Lowestoft. The line north of Beccles, which had carried the direct service to Yarmouth this way, had been discontinued by then and lifted. Today the DMUs run on a single line only, but had Gerard Fiennes, when GM of the Eastern, not thwarted Fred Margetts at HQ it wouldn't be there at all. It is plagued by crossings, which Parish Councils refuse to allow to be closed. C5725

Above **Wickham Market, Suffolk; Class 37, Liverpool Street-Lowestoft, 13 July 1963.**
'For Campsie Ash' read the timetable by way of apology for its 3 miles from the market town. Until 1952 you changed here for Framlingham – note the island platform. Goods trains continued to run there until 1965, however, and I recall standing at the junction that day admiring the Great Eastern lower-quadrants guarding the branch but not taking a picture because they would be there another time. I soon learned the folly of that argument; the film is the cheapest part of an outing. C5726

Below **Saxmundham, Suffolk; DMU, Ipswich-Aldeburgh, 13 July 1963.**
Just look at the substantial water tank to replenish the steam engines on this hilly route. If you turn round you will see the subject of the next picture. C5727

Above **Saxmundham, Suffolk; Class 37, Lowestoft-Liverpool Street, 13 July 1963.**

In the distance can be seen the junction for the branch to Aldeburgh about to be taken by the DMU in the previous picture. I have yet to photograph that – there is an overbridge just to the north – for it is retained to enable the nuclear flask to go to and from Leiston and Sizewell Power Station. C5728

Below **Halesworth, Suffolk; Class 37, Lowestoft-Liverpool Street, 13 July 1963.**

The narrow-gauge Southwold Railway closed as long ago as 1929. I was surprised to find that the waitresses in the hotel here all came from the Far East. C5737

Left Ashwell, Hertfordshire; Class 23 No D5900, 3.19pm Royston-King's Cross, 19 November 1960.

We've now moved west, and this line has been transformed. It is now electrified on the AC overhead system and carries the principal service from London to Cambridge and King's Lynn. This is concentrated on King's Cross and there is a non-stop train nearly every half-hour in addition to local services. It is a different world from the one when I joined the 3.30pm Buffet Car Express from Cambridge as an airman on a 36-hour pass. *AL1194*

Below left Shepreth Branch Junction, Cambridgeshire; Class 31 No D5675, Cambridge-King's Cross (2B66).

Despite the 'change of priority' just mentioned, the junction with the older line from Liverpool Street just outside Cambridge still bears this historic name as far as I know, recalling when it was indeed just a short agricultural branch. *C5369*

Above right Long Stanton (closed 1970), Cambridgeshire; Class 31 No D5622, Wisbech-Cambridge, 23 March 1963.

When privatisation occurred the trackbed here was retained by the remnants of British Rail and sold to Cambridgeshire County Council with a view to re-opening and helping to alleviate road congestion in the city. But nothing appears to have happened. A single line remains under the weeds and perhaps there is a future. The local service normally linked Cambridge, St Ives, March and Wisbech with 'express' trains passing through to and from Kettering until 1959. *2849*

Right Isleham (closed 1962), Cambridgeshire; railbus, Mildenhall-Cambridge, 21 March 1962.

This picture brings back two memories. When I ran railway weekend schools at Madingley Hall near Cambridge we always had an outing in a coach from here and ended up having tea in the bus garage. One of the earliest pictures to stimulate my interest in railways was taken by Pat Whitehouse at Fordham, the intersection of this branch with the Ely-Newmarket line, and now hangs in my entrance hall. What a lovely evening at Isleham, and a Great Eastern signal! I wonder what those at the American Air Force base at Mildenhall thought of the British transport system they saw. *C5693*

Above Barrowden, Northamptonshire; DMU, 8.45am Birmingham (New Street)-Peterborough, 18 September 1964.
The station was Wakerley & Barrowden (left of the signal box) and closed in 1966. The smart train is newly introduced – the dawn of the diesels! C3889

Below Wells-next-the-Sea (closed 1964), Norfolk; DMU from Norwich, 8 August 1964.
A not very inspiring picture, but all I have of this coastal terminus to which trains also came from Heacham (see below) via Burnham Market until 1952. There is now a narrow gauge railway to the outskirts of Wells along the trackbed from Walsingham. C5851

Wymondham, Norfolk; Class 31, Ely-Norwich, 26 March 1966.
This is still an important station, with trains from Norwich to such far distant places as Liverpool and Nottingham, and autumn 2002 saw the much publicised re-introduction of a through service to Cambridge. If I understand the position correctly, this utilises train-sets from elsewhere (perhaps from the Norwich-Basingstoke service, now discontinued) and existing track, signalling and platforms at both ends. Yet the cost is unbelievable. Why? C5830

Below Narborough & Pentney (closed 1968), Norfolk; DMU, King's Lynn-Norwich, 11 May 1968.
I'm told a bypass now occupies the trackbed and brings relief to the villages. At least some good has come from the closure, although as discussed elsewhere this should not have been allowed to happen. C5656

Bottom Wolferton (closed 1969), Norfolk; DMU, King's Lynn-Hunstanton, 11 May 1968.
The Royal Train has long ceased to bring the Queen here for Sandringham, but who would have thought when I took this picture that the train itself might be doomed? Another station for Sandringham was provided by the Midland & Great Northern Joint Railway at Hillington (closed 1959), and this was used as late as 1953 at the time of the flooding of the former GER track near King's Lynn. There is a familiar ring to a journey by the Prince of Wales (later King Edward VII) to Cromer in 1887 when special arrangements had to be made for the Royal party's safety as it was a time of serious trouble in Ireland. C5900

Right Heacham (closed 1969), Norfolk; DMU, Hunstanton-King's Lynn, 10 September 1964.
The branch was still in place for Burnham Market (closed to goods three months later) when this picture was taken, and the formation from King's Lynn is still double track. Just look at all the stored wagons made surplus by the growth of road haulage and the uncertainty as to the future of rail freight, which, unbelievably, continues to this day. C5907

Below right Snettisham (closed 1969), Norfolk; DMU, King's Lynn-Hunstanton, 11 May 1968.
This picture was taken during a weekend stay at The George in Swaffham, to which I had come from taking photographs in Abingdon and along the Bletchley-Bedford line. Indeed, I had lunched at The Rose Revived at Newbridge. Extraordinary! Those with an eye for detail will have noticed that earlier on this Saturday I had been at Middle Drove and Narborough. C5902

Hunstanton (closed 1969), Norfolk; DMU, 5.11pm to March, 10 September 1964.
The end of the line, and quite a substantial station to which Summer Saturday trains came from the East Midlands. C5907

Above Stamford Junction, Lincolnshire; Class 27, Peterborough-Leicester, 14 November 1964.

An interesting view – do notice the ex-Midland double-arm signal and the track crossing over to the branch to the ECML at Essendine, which had come out of the nearby terminus. We ran a special across this one Sunday in 1957 behind a 'C12' Class locomotive bound for Market Harborough and the Leicestershire coalfield. *3346*

Below Barkston East Junction, Lincolnshire; Class 25, Nottingham-Skegness (1E91), 10 July 1965.

This junction can only be reached by track across neighbouring fields, and the farmer has posted 40mph signs for the signalman to observe. When this picture was taken the north curve (to the right) was still in being and used to turn locomotives from Doncaster being tested after overhaul. Until recently plans were afoot to install a curve at Allington (the far end of the Grantham avoiding line from which the train has come) so that the DMUs that currently have to run along the East Coast Main Line can be diverted. Then the track to the left (now a single line) would probably have been lifted and the junction would have disappeared. *3475*

Left Caythorpe (closed 1962), Lincolnshire; DMU, Lincoln Central-Grantham (at 6.37pm), 11 August 1962.

This was reached by a junction at Honington just east of Barkston, and the line ran along under the shelf of the hills to the east. This meant that some of the stations were badly sited for the villages above, and the bus to Lincoln was more convenient. *2734*

Below left Sleaford, Lincolnshire; DMU to Lincoln, 29 May 1967.

Harry and I have just alighted from the 5.07pm from Lincoln and await the 6.05 to Grantham for the express to King's Cross. It is the Spring Bank Holiday and we had spent the Sunday night in Bradford and Saturday night in Shrewsbury, having reached there by the Central Wales Line on the 6.55pm from Llanelly. In between we had visited Blackpool and heard Reginald Dixon play the Wurlitzer organ in the Tower Ballroom. On the Monday we had walked between the stations in Gainsborough. What happy times! *C5995*

Above right Lowdham, Nottinghamshire; DMU, Derby-Lincoln (St Marks), and Class 'B1' 4-6-0 No 61318, Cleethorpes-Exmouth, 11 August 1962.

Do notice the co-acting signal to allow visibility both above and below the bridge on which I am standing, and the adjacent level crossing. This remains a busy line and I often take my picnic lunch here. *2724*

Right Rolleston Junction, Nottinghamshire; DMU, Nottingham (Midland)-Lincoln (St Marks), 1 September 1963.

On the same line but further east this was the point at which you changed for Southwell (until 1959) and Mansfield (until 1929). It is the station for Southwell Racecourse, reached by very secondary roads. A spur at Fiskerton to the west used to bypass both stations to reach the Mansfield line. *C4957*

Left Bardney (closed 1970), Lincolnshire; DMUs, Firsby-Sheffield and Lincoln-Tumby Woodside (really?).
I cannot trace the date of this rather unassuming picture. Until 1951 from here you could have taken the branch over the Wolds to Louth. Trains ran this way from London to York via Boston before the ECML came into existence. C6029

Below left New Bolingbroke (closed 1970), Lincolnshire; DMU, Firsby-Lincoln (Central), 16 August 1969.
Do notice the somersault signals identifying the line as of Great Northern origin. The station is still lit by oil lamps and I suspect the gates have to be opened by hand. I first came this way on a train from Manchester to Skegness, which I joined at Retford 'upstairs' where this route intersected the ECML. This seems a useful point to insert a handbill (*right*) for excursions to Skegness from Leicester (Belgrave Road), which was retained just for these summer weekends. 3664

PLEASE RETAIN THIS BILL FOR REFERENCE   L185/R(HD)

CHEAP TRIPS
TO
SKEGNESS
SUNDAYS
18th JUNE until 10th SEPTEMBER inclusive 1961

FROM	TIMES OF DEPARTURE	RETURN FARES Second Class	ARRIVAL TIMES ON RETURN
	am	s d	pm
LEICESTER Belgrave Road ...	10 22	13/3	10 18
HUMBERSTONE ...	10 28	13/3	10 12
THURNBY & SCRAPTOFT ...	10 34	13/3	10 5
MELTON MOWBRAY North	11 6	10/9	9 33
	pm	Passengers return same day at ...	pm
SKEGNESS ... ... arrive	1 13		7 21

CHILDREN under three years of age, free ; three years and under fourteen, half-fares (fractions of 1d. to be reckoned as 1d.).

RAIL TICKETS CAN BE OBTAINED IN ADVANCE AT STATIONS AND OFFICIAL RAILWAY AGENTS

Further information will be supplied on application to Stations, Official Railway Agents, or to Mr. D. BEATTIE, District Commercial Manager, Leicester. Telephone 23841, Extn. 34.

June 1961
BR 35000
LONDON MIDLAND
(PX3/Halfex/Reg)
Arthur Gaunt & Sons (Printers) Ltd., Hoxton, Derbyshire.

Below Firsby (closed 1970), Lincolnshire; DMU from Lincoln shunting to return there, 16 August 1969.
The excursion from Leicester would have bypassed this station to the south (on the only line that now remains). It was the junction for the north curve from Skegness and served the main line from Grimsby to Peterborough and King's Cross. There is a picture of the Skegness-Bradford train here on the back cover. Note the somersault signal yet again. C6078

Above Willoughby (closed 1970), Lincolnshire; DMU, Grimsby-Peterborough, 16 August 1969.

Just two stations north was another junction in the heart of rural country serving the branch to Mablethorpe (which continued back to the main line at Louth until 1960). There is a connection in the bay hidden on the right-hand side of the picture. C6084

Below Sutton on Sea (closed 1970), Lincolnshire; DMU, Willoughby-Mablethorpe, 16 August 1969.

The connection has emerged from the bay to face the camera here and the somersault signals tell the driver he can go on his way. The children will be getting excited as they spy the sea on their right. C6090

Above Alford (closed 1970), Lincolnshire; DMU, Grimsby-Peterborough, 16 August 1969.

Posters used to invite you to come here by train to see the birthplace of the poet Alfred Lord Tennyson. You can see what a straight main line this used to be across Lincolnshire, and the alternative journey now via Lincoln and Sleaford or Newark is a travesty. *3665*

Below Kirton Lindsey Tunnel, Humberside; DMU, Cleethorpes-Retford, 16 August 1969.

The fine masonry portal of this tunnel could be seen for miles along the straight line from Gainsborough when sitting in the front of what is now described as a Heritage DMU, and it seemed to draw the train like a pin to a magnet. The station man has given me permission to trespass here, having watched the Skegness-Manchester hurry through his station. Today the Manchester, Sheffield & Lincolnshire main line (subsequently Great Central) is here a single track, and passenger trains run only on Saturdays, which I suspect is still questionable in legal circles. Thus Kirton Lindsey – and, more important perhaps, the tourist centre of Brigg – have three trains each way a week. *3667*

Above Barnetby, Humberside; DMU to Cleethorpes, 29 May 1967.

We are on our way to Sleaford (see page 76 above). This must be the most visited station in the provinces by enthusiasts anxious to photograph the variety of freight trains that pass through here to and from Immingham. Wrawby Junction remains nearby with its range of semaphore signals still in daily use, as well as those we can see in the picture. The station buildings have recently been replaced. *C6242*

Below Hornsea (closed 1964), Humberside; DMU to Hull, 4 January 1964.

We've crossed the Humber now and by the East Coast it is a typically misty winter morning. Actually, I feel it gives the picture an added dimension because you can almost feel the cold. I had travelled to Hull the previous evening on the Pullman from King's Cross and stayed in The Station Hotel, which was nice and warm. I made the journey just for this picture in anticipation of the closure the following October. *C6385*

Above right Burton Agnes (closed 1970), Humberside; DMU, Scarborough-Hull, August 1969.

The line from Hull to Scarborough has been luckier than that to Hornsea, thanks to the efforts of people like Ken Dodd, but not this station, which might have been kept for tourists to the famous house nearby. True, it's a generous half-mile away, but that's all right on a fine day. Isn't it? *C6418*

Right Bridlington, Humberside; DMU to Hull, August 1969.

What a fine array of signals, most of them of North Eastern Railway origin. And look at the sidings provided to cope with the numerous excursions from other parts of the network. I suspect that people now commute from here to Hull. *C6419*

Above Market Weighton (closed 1965), Humberside; DMU, Hull-York, 1 May 1964.

I would never have believed that a train service connecting two important cities, with Pocklington, here and Beverley in between, could possibly have been closed. The potential was significant, with much housing development in the 1960s and commuting both ways. As Mackenzie, one-time GM of the successful Southdown Buses used to say, 'Anchor a route in a town at both ends and there will always be passengers'. Someone at York HQ had not learned that, and I suspect promotion depended on savings rather than initiative. Isn't the lighting of the picture fascinating? You could change here for Selby and Driffield on the intersecting route. *C6391*

Above right Hunmanby, North Yorkshire; DMU, Hull-Scarborough, 6 April 1968.

South of the station a single line now runs to Bridlington. I'm spending a long weekend B&B at Egton station, sleeping there above the former booking office and being shaken awake by the newspaper train hurrying through around 6 o'clock in the morning from Darlington to Whitby. The owner was very proud of her son-in-law (I think), who had begun to write successful novels under the name of Nicholas Rhea, and which formed the basis of the popular TV series *Heartbeat*. Hunmanby has prospered too, and is now quite a sizeable community. *C6439*

Right Ravenscar (closed 1965), North Yorkshire; DMU, Middlesbrough-Scarborough, 2 May 1964.

This famous view has appeared often on posters, leaflets and in magazines, and is almost at the summit of the climb from Robin's Hood Bay, which is featured in the background. The summit is in the nearby tunnel, which was created at the whim of the local landowner and was low and very damp. Frank Young, an experienced and kindly engine-driver from Malton, recalled the day that he had to pilot a circular tour excursion from Leeds up this bank. He had advised the driver of the main train to open up his locomotive as they passed the brickyard, and under no circumstances to relax until they entered the tunnel when he must shut off. But his advice was not followed with the result that the train not only stalled in the tunnel but came out the way it had gone in. Back to the bottom and a second try, which was successful, but Frank refused to pilot the man from Scarborough back to York! *3146*

Above left Prospect Hill, Whitby, North Yorkshire; DMU, 12.50pm Middlesbrough-Scarborough, 26 February 1965.
The approach to Whitby from Scarborough was unique. First the train ran over the viaduct above the Esk Valley Line, then it passed this signal box to enter West Cliff Station. After reversal it returned beneath the signal box and went down the bank to Bog Hall (below), where it joined the metals that had come under the viaduct and entered the terminus. Meanwhile on the right folk played rugby. C6708

Left Bog Hall, Whitby, North Yorkshire; DMU, Middlesbrough-Scarborough, 2 May 1964.
It's a murky day, but the turntable is visible and the carriage sidings, while in the background an excursion is waiting to return to somewhere with rain-sodden passengers. Look at the size of the water tank to replenish all those engines that come here. A North Eastern signal completes the scene. You may be able to see Whitby Abbey on the far side of the river. C6729

Above Whitby Town, North Yorkshire; DMU, 3.58pm to York, 26 February 1965.
I make no apology for including a disproportionate number of photos of this area, as I feel it is so interesting. We've now reached the terminus, which survives and has been renovated despite losing the services to Malton and Scarborough in 1965. Whitby seems to be a location that worries Ministers of the Crown. Ernest Marples, as Minister of Transport and founder of the road construction business of Marples, Ridgeway & Partners, in which he retained shares until 1960 (when they were transferred to Nutraco Nominees Ltd, according to *The Railway Gazette*), seemed determined to close the railways to Whitby and rejected every appeal to the contrary, despite their great value in the snowy conditions of the East Coast and their tourist potential. Only the bridge at Glaisdale and the need to educate children saved the Esk Valley. The M11 has yet to be extended up the coast. Then, when local government re-organisation was predicted in 1969 and Whitby was destined to join Teesside, it was the presence of local fisherwomen with an outdated catch sitting outside the Department in London for days that led to second thoughts. C6716

Above left Kirkbymoorside (closed 1953), North Yorkshire; 9.40am Ramblers' DMU from Bradford (Forster Square), 3 May 1964.
I had no idea at the time that I would come to live near and shop here on a regular basis. The premises are now used by agricultural engineers and the building survives. It could not have been better sited for the town and many still regret the loss of their link to York and cheap evening trips to Scarborough. My village had its own station, but had it retained the trains I suspect that by now we would be a commuter suburb. C6595

Left Grosmont, North Yorkshire; Class 40 No D355, 4.20pm Malton-Whitby, 14 September 1964.
This is now the junction of the North Yorkshire Moors Railway and its preserved trains from Pickering with the Esk Valley Line service from Middlesbrough to Whitby run by Arriva. The signal box has gone. When I stayed at Egton it was operated by the tenant who lived there. C6772

Top Glaisdale, North Yorkshire; DMU, Middlesbrough-Whitby, 5 April 1968.
This station has retained its loop, albeit without semaphores; instead, there is electrical token signalling from Battersby and Whitby respectively, although Grosmont can be brought into use when the NYMR needs access. Do notice the handsome bracket post and siding control, and the tangerine sign of the North Eastern Region. C6772

Above Castleton, North Yorkshire; DMUs, Middlesbrough-Scarborough and vice versa, 4 August 1963.
A family are making their way to the seaside at a station that has since lost its passing loop. I'm on my way from Selby to Newcastle, having already travelled via Market Weighton, Scarborough and Whitby and going ahead to Saltburn and Darlington as well as Whitley Bay. My homeward journey next day takes in Wetherby, the Spen Valley Line west from Leeds, Penistone and Retford. C6833

Above Battersby, North Yorkshire; DMU, Middlesbrough-Scarborough, 4 August 1963.

The destination indicators are in NER tangerine. Note the junction signals; since closure of the direct line from Stockton via Picton in 1954, all trains reverse here. Some American friends remarked that there now seemed no reason for this, as a direct north-to-east curve could be constructed across a nearby field. I had to tell them that capital work would be involved, and that this was penurious England. C6859

Below Great Ayton, North Yorkshire; DMU, Whitby-Middlesbrough, 25 May 1966.

In the best North Eastern tradition the now disused yard contains a ramp from which wagons discharged coal into the lorries below. Today this village contains much-sought-after property and is home to the middle classes of Teesside. How many commute by train I know not. C6872

Above Crag Hall, Cleveland; Class 27 No D5378, southbound freight, 4 December 1964.
The locomotive is assisted by a brake tender, and in the foreground is the 'pulpit' on which the signalman stands to exchange the token for the single-line sections. Until 1958 this line provided an alternative route from Teesside to Whitby, but now it is cut back to the Boulby Potash Mine. Some bridges over the roads have been rebuilt and the future seems secure; there is much heavy freight traffic to photograph. C6704

Below Saltburn, Cleveland; three DMUs, 15 January 1967.
The Zetland Hotel had direct access from the platform when I last stayed here, but that was a long time ago. My bedroom contained some beautiful woodwork and the waitresses were of an age to defer to their visitors. Saltburn is currently restoring itself to some of its former glory. Fortunately the heavy freight to Boulby bypasses most of the resort. C7190

Above Thornaby, Tees Yard, Cleveland; DMU, Darlington-Saltburn, 28 May 1965.
A product of the BR Modernisation Plan of 1955, this yard shows the prototype view with the passenger train skirting round the edge. C7177

Below Billingham Beck branch, Cleveland; Class 40, Liverpool-Newcastle, 13 June 1965.
A Sunday diversion due to engineering work. C7268

Above Middlesbrough, Cleveland; Class 25 with brake tender and freight, 28 May 1965.
Do notice the gas holders and, in between them, the transporter bridge, now restored and re-opened to road traffic. *C7178*

Below Eaglescliffe, Cleveland; two southbound DMUs bound for York and Darlington respectively, 4 August 1965.
The western edge of Teesside; 19th-century houses on one side, fields on the other. *C7170*

Billingham Old Station, Cleveland; DMU, Middlesbrough-Newcastle, 26 August 1964.
The old goods yard on the left, new houses on the right. C7275

Hartlepool, Cleveland; Class 40, Liverpool-Newcastle, 13 June 1965.
Industry everywhere. The train is a far cry from the two- or three-coach units that make the itinerary now. C7267

Brompton (closed 1965), North Yorkshire; DMU, 7.55am Leeds-West Hartlepool, 20 November 1964.

This picture provides memories of the time when this was part of the Leeds Northern Railway had through trains via Ripon (closed 1967). It united with what has become the East Coast Main Line through Northallerton and resulted in the construction by the station there of County Hall for North Yorkshire, whose writ now runs as far west as Settle. Passenger services became very sparse through Brompton, although the 'Cleveland Executive' HST ran this way from King's Cross. Freight continued unabated, however, with delays to road traffic at level crossings both north and, on the station avoiding line, south of Northallerton. And today there is again a regular passenger service between Manchester Airport and Middlesbrough, augmented by trains from York up the coast. C7130

Yarm Viaduct, North Yorkshire; DMU to Middlesbrough, 25 June 1966.
This carries the line over the River Leven, which forms a horseshoe round the town, and runs behind the shops on the west side of the attractive market area. It is built of brick except the most northerly arch, which is in stone and bears an inscription. C7149

High Dyke, Lincolnshire; Class 31, up parcels, 3 May 1970.
The train has been climbing up from the Trent Valley since Newark and is now nearing the summit, which is in Stoke Tunnel just to the right of my feet. In the background are the sidings at High Dyke, which contain loaded wagons and provide access to the main line from the quarries at Stainby (page 4). That traffic has now ceased, but not without leaving a useful bridge for the landowner over the updated A1 nearby. *5398*

Grantham, Lincolnshire; Class 47, up 'Tees-Tyne Pullman' (1E08), 5 September 1964.
We are at the birthplace of Baroness Thatcher, and a town that the present Government has in mind to enlarge to provide more housing for the South East! There is capacity on the railway to London and the journey takes only about an hour. Ideal! But not by Pullman. I wonder where those spotters are now? I've changed here to go to Lincoln, there to join a Summer Saturday Yarmouth-Manchester, which I will leave at Penistone for another, Bournemouth-Leeds/Bradford (Exchange), and spend the night at the Midland Hotel. It is Denby Dale Pie Day and the long train proves a godsend for those hurrying to leave the event in a sudden cloudburst. *5404*

Left Nottingham (Victoria) (closed 1967), Nottinghamshire; Class 47, Bournemouth-Newcastle, 7 August 1965.
I would not have obtained this photograph had the express not been late. I've come from Marylebone and our train was given precedence over this one at Culworth Junction (title page). What a barn of a place, in what looked like a quarry! The wind blew through the tunnels at each end and dust and soot was everywhere. But it had far more character than the supermarket that has replaced it. *4229*

Below Barlborough, Nottinghamshire; Class 31, Sheffield-Skegness (1K26), 11 July 1964.
I came along here in my train from Lincoln referred to on the previous page. It was part of the Lancashire, Derbyshire & East Coast Railway built early in the 20th century, but has been abandoned here and remains only as a supply route to the High Marnham Power Station, which is used only to supplement the grid when necessary. *4341*

Above right Upton Magna (closed 1963), Salop; Class 47, 'Pines Express' Bournemouth-Liverpool/Manchester (1M04), 23 April 1966.
It was strange that at the time the 'Pines Express' only came this way via Shrewsbury on Saturdays – midweek it went direct from Wellington to Nantwich by way of Coole Pilot Halt. Note the Wrekin in the background round which we are alleged to run! *2757*

Below **Craven Arms, Salop; Class 47, Liverpool-Penzance (1V92), 17 July 1965.**

The first time I went to Craven Arms was on 2 July 1956. I had to drive from my B&B in All Stretton because there was no connection, and joined the 6.59am to Swansea (Victoria) from the bay on the left of this picture, then the Mumbles Tram back to Mumbles Road Station for the 12.34pm that returned me to Builth Road (High Level). From the Low Level I went north to Moat Lane Junction on the 2.45, coming back on the 5.30. A lady also joined the train at Mumbles Road and travelled with me to Moat Lane, going on to Forden (closed 1965) to visit a relative in the mental hospital there. Real devotion! And last but not least I boarded the 7.04pm to Craven Arms (which originated at Llandovery) and was made up of those corridor coaches that have two sliding doors to enclose each compartment, often obstructed by a discarded cigarette packet. It was sunny all day and I have the happiest memories of this, my first journey across the Principality. At Bucknell we seemed to be waiting a long time, and I found the driver, fireman and guard on the station seat sunning themselves. They told me that they exchanged crews here with a westbound goods, and when this arrived I was on my way once more – still with the train to myself. I can see the goods coming up the line even now, yet didn't bother to photograph it because I thought it would be there for ever. *2882*

Above **Bunbury, Cheshire; Class 40, Bangor-Birmingham (New Street) (1G10), 15 May 1966.**
I have driven here from Crewe, having sailed overnight from Northern Ireland and via the Heysham-Euston boat train, on which I have had breakfast. Unbeknown to me, my friend John Edgington was waiting at Crewe to take this train to Birmingham. There is a good weekday service between Crewe and Chester, one an hourly shuttle and the other, sometimes regularly a Class 47 and Mk 2 stock, going on along the North Wales coast. *4060*

Below **Leigh (closed 1966), Staffordshire; DMU, Derby-Crewe, 6 May 1961.**
This station served a very small community way off the main road. On driving away we came upon a road junction with a 'Halt' sign separated from us by a ford across a stream. We were spending a weekend at Hoar Cross. *4285*

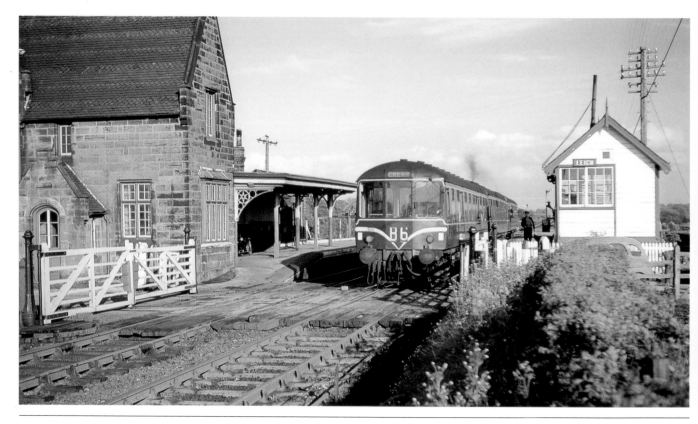

Hathersage, Derbyshire; Class 31, westbound freight (9M90), 17 July 1964. I think this a splendid picture taken in the late afternoon, and well deserves full-page treatment. The hill in the background separates us from Sheffield and the main road climbs out of the Hope Valley at this point to go over the top. The railway continues to Grindleford and through the lengthy Totley Tunnel. The station buildings have been demolished but there is a two-hourly-interval service calling here. 5161

Stocksmoor, West Yorkshire; DMU, Huddersfield-Penistone, 3 May 1963.
Since its reduction to single track this station has grown in importance as the one with a loop to enable the regular-interval services to pass each other, usually at a quarter to the hour. Most trains go through to Lincoln, whereas when this picture was taken they terminated shortly at Penistone (or went to Clayton West). Do notice the backing plate on the signal in the foreground to facilitate sighting and the early design of the paintwork on the train. 4518

Above Brockholes, West Yorkshire; Class 45 Leeds/Bradford-Bournemouth (1O43), 22 July 1967.

The millstone paving and gas light date this picture, and trains of this nature no longer pass this way on the surviving single track. The woods on the left are famous for their carpet of bluebells. *4521*

Below Entwhistle, Lancashire; DMU, Bolton-Blackburn, 14 April 1967.

An extraordinary layout! Non-stop trains passed by under the signal box while those that deigned to call used the island platform. Mustn't the signal box be draughty – how did you keep your feet warm in there? A good position for a bird-watcher. Today there is just a single line at this point linking Bromley Cross with Darwen. *8339*

Above Grange-over-Sands, Cumbria; Class 24, westbound route-learning special (4F00), 29 August 1969.
This is the only occasion on which I have seen a learner driver with his own ECS. The promenade here was laid out by the Furness Railway with gardens the other side of the line and an agreement made with the local authority to maintain them. As far as I know this still exists, for the place is kept clean and tidy by Council staff. It is a joy to be there – sun and sea views and passing trains with signals to tell you when they are coming. 9473

Below Carlisle, Cumbria; DMU to Silloth, 26 March 1964.
We're at the north end of Citadel station and the train uses the

Caledonian to reach the North British branch line. It's a very pleasant ride with views out of the front. 9704

Right Silloth (closed 1964), Cumbria; Class 26 No D5310, 6.00pm to Carlisle, 6 September 1964.
Closure was imminent when this picture was taken. I have written about the location above (page 58). 9721

Below right Glenwhilly (closed 1965), Dumfries & Galloway; DMU, Glasgow (St Enoch)-Stranraer, 14 July 1966.
By now you won't be surprised to learn that I really enjoy visits to this lonely location, reached only by a track from the narrow lane that links New Luce with Barrhill, which is much shorter than the railway as the line has to circumnavigate the hills. I had taken the car by Motorail from London to Newcastle (in company with John Mills, the actor and his two dogs) with lunch on board, and had driven across, picking up Ian Cantlon in Carlisle. We spent the weekend at the nearby Glentuchar Hotel. After dinner on the Friday we passed a very pleasant time at Barrhill station where northbound trains were block to block (ie Glenwhilly and Pinwherry) following the arrival of the boat from Northern Ireland. By this time the direct route to Dumfries through Newton Stewart had been closed, so there came not only a Glasgow train and a relief but also the Euston-bound sleeper. A southbound service just had to wait. There is talk of transferring the boat from Stranraer to Troon, in which case the future of this line must be in doubt if the peace process consolidates. The signalman is exchanging tokens for the single line. 9840

Fairlie High, Strathclyde; DMU, Largs-Glasgow, 27 August 1965.
One can obviously make jokes about the name, for the station is indeed on high ground. As the distant signal bears witness, there was a junction at the far end of the tunnel with a branch to Fairlie Pier, now lifted. Electric trains now run this way but only on one line. so I understand. *9920*

Near Abington, Strathclyde; Class 40, up 'Royal Scot', 21 May 1964.
We're on the way from Douglas to Kilmarnock. It's a nice day, so why not stay on the West Coast Main Line for a few hours? *10049*

Falahill, Borthwick Bank, Lothian; Class 40, Edinburgh (Millerhill)-Carlisle freight (4M64), 2 September 1965.
Will this line be restored as far as Hawick and between the forests at Steele Road and Carlisle? I wait to see. Its closure in 1969 was incredible, but it ran through constituencies held by the Liberal Party, which may have been relevant. More likely Beeching saw it as a duplicate route between Edinburgh and Carlisle, despite the fact that the West Coast Main Line serves only Lockerbie (occasionally), whereas this route ran through the substantial township of Galashiels (with Selkirk nearby) and Hawick. Ian is in the foreground taking his picture. There seems no shortage of freight this morning, and I expect the driver is glad he is nearing the top of the bank. The signal box must derive its name from the hamlet of Fala, 3 miles away. *10270*

Below Scarborough, North Yorkshire; DMU to Middlesbrough, 4 March 1965.
What a fine station this is, and much of it has been restored, although rationalisation has enabled the south side to be used for parking. The trains to Middlesbrough used to move just out of the station, then change direction through a tunnel to head for Whitby. The turntable was restored at the will of the ratepayers during the celebrations to mark the 50th anniversary of *Mallard*'s record-breaking run, and now steam trains often run here from York and beyond. 6660

Bottom Egton, North Yorkshire; DMU to Whitby, 5 April 1969.
This was my base for so many happy weekends, which led to my retirement to this part of the country. I used to sleep above the bow window. At the time of my first visit there was a short-working from Whitby to Glaisdale on a Saturday evening, which returned empty stock. My host was then the guard (later signalman at Grosmont) and invited me to join the train after dinner, just for the ride. On the return the train made a special stop to put me down. Such simple events are the source of really happy memories. 6793

Right North Queensferry, Fife; Class 40, Aberdeen-Edinburgh (Waverley), 28 August 1965.
We are in Scotland now, and the train is climbing from Inverkeithing up to the Forth Bridge; note the earthworks in the form of the cutting and embankment that this necessitated. Hitherto the train had been ferried across from Burntisland to Granton. I'm waiting for the preserved locomotive *Glen Douglas* to come the other way on a special to the Fife coast and Newburgh, then returning via Glen Farg. 10309

Below right Lunan Bay (station closed 1930), Tayside; Class 40, Aberdeen-Edinburgh, 26 May 1966.
I'm driving from Carnoustie to Stonehaven, taking in Forfar on the way, for pictures on both main lines before the Strathmore route closed a year later. There is a storm brewing over the sea. 10553

Above Ballater (closed 1966), Grampian; DMU to Aberdeen, 7 June 1965.

There was much surprise when closure was announced, for the Royal Train came here on a regular basis to bring the Queen to Balmoral. Wolferton, for Sandringham (page 72), was also to lose its service four years later. Now the actual train is threatened. For some time a battery-operated unit was used here, but apparently it was not a success. *10696*

Below Bannockburn, Central; Class 29 No D6101, Glasgow (Buchanan Street)-Dundee, 23 May 1966.

We're staying in Stirling, and earlier in the day we had made a journey by rail using the 10.08am to Dundee, the 12.18pm to Thornton Junction, the 1.15 to Dunfermline and the 2.08 back to Stirling via Alloa, which was to close in 1968. After this picture we moved to see the TPO come the other way (page 111 below). *10468*

Above Hilton Tunnel, Perth, Tayside; Class 45, Glasgow (Buchanan Street)-Dundee, 25 May 1966.
Two days later we are here, having spent the morning travelling by the goods from Perth to Crieff via Methven Junction and returning on the 12.05pm bus. We then moved on to Alyth and Carnoustie, where our friends failed to turn up because they had misunderstood the date of our rendezvous. Disappointment! At the far end of the tunnel is the junction for Newburgh and Ladybank. *10508*

Below Glen Ogle Viaduct, Central; Class 27, 12.40pm Oban-Glasgow (Buchanan Street), 29 June 1965.
The Callander & Oban Railway was closed between Dunblane and Crianlarich in 1965 and trains concentrated on the line to Fort William above the shores of Loch Lomond. There was said to be an earthslip in the region of this viaduct, which precipitated early withdrawal of the trains. *11459*

Above Ballachulish (closed 1966), Highland; Class 27, 4.10pm to Oban, 22 August 1964.

This branch left the Oban line at Connel Ferry, where it used to share the bridge with road traffic. I believe that the highway has now been diverted on to the former railway bridge at Creagan too. Kentallen station used to boast a shop and tearoom and adjoin a pier for steamer trips on Loch Linnhe. *11520*

Below Achnasheen, Highland; Class 26 No D5341, Inverness-Kyle of Lochalsh, 25 August 1965.

It was not unknown for the train crew to down a dram in the station refreshment room while they awaited the service the other way. Perhaps they still do. For years dining cars were conveyed from Inverness and exchanged here to make the return journey. *10992*

Thirsk, North Yorkshire; Class 45 Newcastle-Paignton (1V87), 13 September 1969.
My friend Cyril joined this train to change at York and go home to London. The main-line sides of the island platforms have now been sealed off, and all trains stop at the outer sides. Sadly almost all the down trains are for Middlesbrough, with a change necessary at Northallerton, the very next station, after barely a 10-minute ride, to go to Darlington, Durham and Newcastle, and connections seem to be arbitrary. Why cannot the DMUs between York and Newcastle call here while there is still space to park? The buildings have been demolished and replaced by new structures, but there is usually staff on duty and the waiting area-cum-ticket office is nice and warm. They will tell you where your train is on their TV monitors, but their phone number is no longer in the BT directory. So much for centralisation! C7050

Northallerton, North Yorkshire; Class 40, down express, 7 March 1964.
A train is signalled to the up local at Longlands Junction where the station bottleneck ends. The photograph is sufficiently old for the signal also to have an indication available for Ripon, Harrogate and Leeds direct (closed 1967). I once joined a DMU in the bay on the left on a Sunday morning to spend the day in the spa town, leaving there later by the 'Harrogate Sunday Pullman' to King's Cross. The keyhole for the booking office door was at ground level, and I recall the difficulty with which the elderly booking clerk got down to insert the key. On the train I alone had dinner in my coach; the main course was sirloin steak. The passenger opposite got out his sandwiches. No wonder the Pullmans were soon withdrawn. But what a pity! C7062

Above Ferryhill, County Durham; Class 55 'Deltic' No D9011, down parcels, 19 December 1965.

The parcels is crossing over to gain access to the platform here (closed two years later). It was also the only way to ensure that further north at Tursdale Junction you could enter the older line via Leamside to Newcastle. On each charter I ran that way we were brought to a stand at the first signal so that special arrangements could be made for our safe passage, as someone had stolen the copper wire integral to the system. In early 2003 thieves actually lifted several miles of track unofficially, cut the rails into short lengths and were about to steal it when discovered. Not the most desirable area to visit! C7569

Below Durham Viaduct, County Durham; Class 40, up express, March 1964.

Yet what could be nicer than a trip to the city of Durham? There are public gardens above the station to the west from which you can gaze down on the railway movements. The cathedral and the university beckon, as do the shops. Pity it is such a climb back to the station. C7607

Above Hexham, Northumberland; DMU to Newcastle Central, 14 July 1966.

I'm driving to Glenwhilly. Do notice that the DMU is conveying a van for the parcels. The 3.40pm from Carlisle used to be a locomotive-hauled train that called only here on its way to Newcastle. I travelled by it quite often and photographed it even more. At one stage it was extended north to Chathill and Berwick. C7640

Below Middleton in Teesdale (closed 1964), County Durham; Ramblers' DMU, 4 July 1964.

This was the end of the branch from Tees Valley Junction, Barnard Castle, on the Stainmore line, and at one time a paradise of flowers in the booking hall and the entrance drive. The cast-iron lamp-post beside my front door is said to come from Romaldkirk on the branch, although the lantern is modern. C7447

Coanwood, Northumberland; DMU, Haltwhistle-Alston, 14 April 1965.
A full page to marvel at the sight of this tall antique signal. The line survived until 1976 because of the difficulty of providing a substitute bus service. In the end a new road bridge had to be built across the Tyne near here to connect Coanwood with Lambley so that the railway could come to an end. Precision Products of Alston, for instance, were forbidden to send their traffic by rail so as to cause more losses. A narrow gauge preservation service – the South Tynedale Railway – now operates at the southern end of the branch. C7668

Above Alnmouth, Northumberland; DMU from Newcastle, 21 May 1966.

It is said that the Alnwick branch may be restored from here, and the continuing influence of the local aristocracy, the fame of the town for tourists and the widening of the A1 bypass, the bridge for which provided the excuse for closure in 1968, may make this a real possibility. Alnmouth station has changed out of all recognition. The 'Royal Scotsman' with its £3,000 price-tag (33 people in a train of eight coaches) sometimes sets down here for a tour of the Duke of Northumberland's estate. It lays over in the Woodenbridge Loop and picks up its patrons at Acklington, the next station south. *C8010*

Below Chathill, Northumberland; Class 55 'Deltic', down express (1A16), 6 September 1968.

This is now the terminus of the evening local from Newcastle, which, until privatisation, continued to Berwick on Tweed. It starts here in the morning, having come empty stock, but because there is no crossover it has to proceed to Belford to start back, and this has caused resentment among residents there who would like the chance to use it, if only their station could be restored. At one time a postbus used to provide a connection to Bamburgh, but I'm not sure whether that is still the case. *C8056*

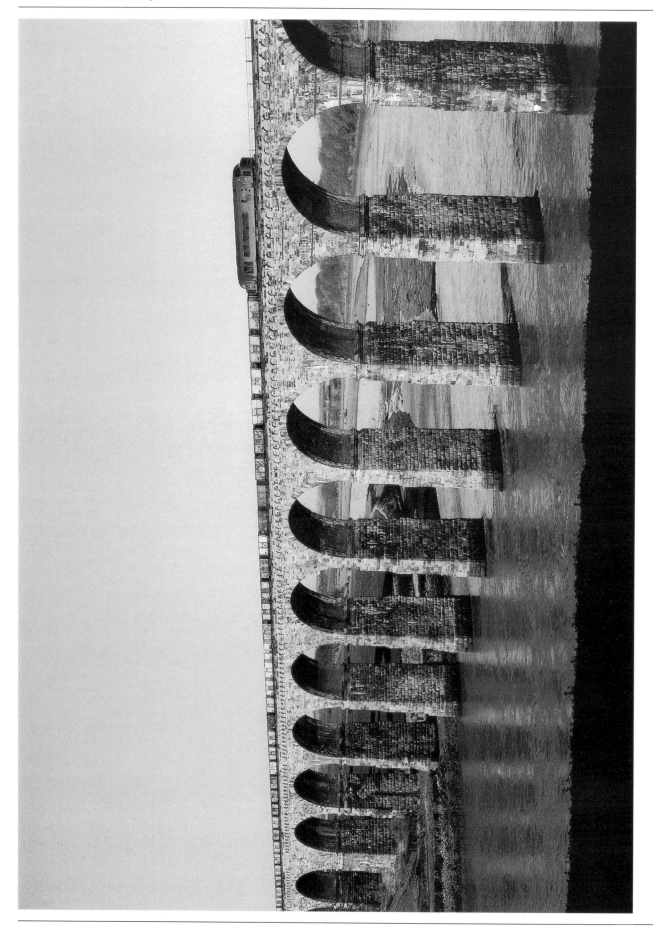

Royal Border Bridge, Berwick on Tweed, Northumberland; Class 46 No D176, down freight, 26 March 1964.
I'm always glad that the relatively new river bridge on the bypass is round the corner out of sight so that we can still enjoy the majesty of this structure.
Even the masts for today's overhead wires were especially designed. C8093

5.
SCOTLAND

And now we come to the last chapter in the book, which suitably opens with a view of probably the most famous train in the world, the 'Flying Scotsman', before it became just another 225 and terminated in Edinburgh rather than Aberdeen as hitherto. It has just entered Scotland at Marshall's Meadows and passengers are enjoying that superb view of the North Sea. Soon they will pass Innerwick, site of the second picture, having bypassed Penmanshiel Tunnel, tomb of those unfortunate men seeking to accommodate larger freight vehicles, then Torness Nuclear Power Station. At Drem they will be joined by the local electric trains that ply between North Berwick and the capital city.

Edinburgh used to be reached (until 1969) also by the Waverley Route from Carlisle via the Border towns. This was a great loss. On the southbound 'Waverley Express' you could take breakfast, lunch, tea and dinner en route. I travelled throughout on Tuesday 31 March 1964, leaving at 10.15am and arriving in London at 8.20pm. It ran over the Settle & Carlisle and eventually terminated at St Pancras, soon to be home to the Channel Tunnel trains. I recall joining a special from Glasgow (18 April 1965), which stated in its prospectus that it would call at Riccarton Junction, a location then almost impossible to reach by road. The weather was perfect and I was looking forward to a photo opportunity when it steamed straight through and called instead at Kershopefoot, which is easily accessible by car. I remonstrated with the organisers who just could not comprehend my annoyance. Geographical knowledge is not a speciality today, as witness University Challenge on TV! I managed to get the car to the junction along a forestry road at a later date.

Another special that originated at Edinburgh (at 8.12am on 25 March 1967) had 18 coaches, I believe, and proved to be an incredible day out behind diesel traction for much of the time. Passage of the Waverley Route to Carlisle was but an aperitif. We then headed back through Coatbridge to Perth, and (with Nos 44997 and 60009 at the head) on via the Caledonian line to Aberdeen. From

Keith we went by way of Craigellachie and the Spey Valley Line – normally restricted to railbuses and closed to passenger traffic in 1965 – to Aviemore. Three locomotives were required to haul the heavy train over the summit and back to Perth. Here the steam locos reappeared as far as Stirling. We terminated in Glasgow at 10.34pm and went straight to bed.

Normally I took the car by Motorail to Scotland, first from King's Cross, then from Caledonian Road to Perth. Later the journey was from Olympia to Inverness, and later still from York, which was perfect. All these ventures were overnight, preceded by dinner, thus gaining time to relax. I hope they may return when the motorways get gridlocked. Just before I owned a car Alan and I made our first visit to Scotland using a Circular Tour Ticket in a booklet with LNER on the cover in 1957. We travelled by the 'Flying Scotsman' on 18 May and saw the Forth Bridge for the first time the next day; a ferry still carried cars across. We went round the Kingdom of Fife through Anstruther to Dundee and on to Aberdeen. Fraserburgh, St Combs and Peterhead were followed by Ballater (and Braemar), then to Pitlochry via the Spey Valley.

There we were looked down upon by the management of Fisher's Hotel for not arriving by car. Aberfeldy, Crieff and Killin read like a forgotten world. Obviously Fort William, Wick, Thurso and the Kyle were followed by the boat trip to Mallaig and hence to Glasgow with Balloch thrown in as a makeweight. The journey back to London was from St Enoch on the 'Thames-Clyde Express', arriving at St Pancras on the Saturday evening a fortnight after we had left. This run, mostly behind steam, facilitated years of pictures from the car thereafter.

On 16 August 1999 I obtained a long-awaited picture west of Scotscalder station, where, at Dornery, a low hill gives a view across the bleak landscape inhabited almost exclusively by the single line to Altnabreac and Forsinard, but it cannot be included here because of the date. This is private land and, having opened and closed a gate, I drove through some farm buildings to the summit. Here I came

Burnmouth, Borders; Class 55 'Deltic', 'Flying Scotsman' King's Cross-Aberdeen, 18 July 1963.
What better way to enter the country than to cross the Royal Border Bridge, pass over the railway boundary at Marshall's Meadows and arrive here by the 'Flying Scotsman' behind a 'Deltic' locomotive. At that time – before electrification – the train went through to Aberdeen. The 10mph sign relates to the crossover that gave entry to the branch to Eyemouth (closed 1962). I was never able to ride this as the service was so poor; indeed, I have no photographs either. C8126

upon a group of shooters dressed in Highland garb, and I thought that I might have caused a problem by disturbing the grouse. One of the party was the laird, and when I explained my purpose he proved to be a reader of Silver Link publications and not only made me welcome but suggested a better vantage point – but mind the car doesn't get stuck in the mud, he said. The DMU looked lost and I hope to go back to see the freight that now runs that way again.

One place I have still to reach, however – and it's not too late provided I have the strength – is the summit of Ravens Rock near Strathpeffer north of Inverness. From here one can look down on the train to the Kyle climbing up from Achterneed, which should be a splendid view. I have walked through the woods from there and have reached the line beneath the bluff, but failed to negotiate it. There must be an easier route. Here's to the next time!

Innerwick, Lothian; Class 47, Cliffe-Uddingston cement, 20 May 1966.
This morning we came from Duns (having stayed overnight) to Reston on the goods, picked up the car and made for North Berwick, where we took the train in and out of Edinburgh, to Corstorphine in fact (closed 1968). On the way we saw this freight, and coming back the 'A4' *Kingfisher* on a special to Newcastle. *C8185*

Hedderwick, Lothian; Class 47, Perth-Holloway Motorail, 20 May 1966.
We also paused here, knowing that this train was due. The vans used to house my Morris Minor in the recess just above track level; they were withdrawn because of staff fatalities, as I understand it. C8190

Above Newcastleton (closed 1969), Borders; Class 45, down
'Waverley Express' St Pancras-Edinburgh (Waverley) (1S64), 5
September 1968.

Now back to the much-lamented Waverley Route with pictures near
each end. By the signboard the postman is waiting with his mailbag,
which contains a film I was sending for processing that I had earlier put
in the box by the Post Office. Later I decided to buy a postcard there
and was surprised when the postmistress commented that I was a long
way from home – in those days one's address was on the film envelope.
She said that the film would first go north to Edinburgh, then up the
East Coast to London. *3648*

Below Tynehead (closed 1969), Lothian; Class 45, up 'Waverley
Express' Edinburgh (Waverley)-St Pancras (1M88), 2 September
1965.

The Post Office here was in the station building and the lady there
insisted, quite rightly, that Ian and I should both buy railway tickets,
which she dated with our respective birthdays. She campaigned for
their one train a day to Edinburgh to be shown in the timetable, but in
vain – only the southbound service appeared. *3522*

Left Currie, Lothian; Class 47 No D1506, up express, 21 May 1966.

This line is shared with the local service to Glasgow via Fauldhouse as far as Midcalder Junction, where the now electrified trains of the East Coast Main Line veer south to Carstairs. West Coast trains come this way too, and no longer have to meet up with a portion from Glasgow as this one will do before proceeding south. *C10090*

Below left Bathgate Junction, Lothian; DMU, Glasgow (Queen Street)-Edinburgh (Waverley), 28 August 1965.

We await here a special with *Glen Douglas* from Glasgow via Bathgate (left) before heading across the Firth of Forth to North Queensferry to see it again there and several times afterwards. *C10149*

Right Pinwherry (closed 1965), Strathclyde; DMU, Glasgow (St Enoch)-Stranraer, 27 August 1965.

Two views on the Stranraer line: this might have been the junction for Ballantrae had plans come to fruition. Instead it remained a loop on the single line. *C9862*

Below Pinmore Viaduct, Strathclyde; DMU, Stranraer-Glasgow (St Enoch), 16 July 1966.

Just south is this viaduct, which, as you can see, had structural problems even then. The main road climbs round under the right-hand arch, but how to get on a level with the line? A number of years afterwards I approached a local farmer and was allowed to come down through his fields, although those pictures are much later than 1970. *3617*

Above Sandilands Viaduct, Strathclyde; DMU, Lanark-Muirkirk, 22 May 1964.

A line that never seemed to get publicity ran from Lanark on the Caledonian to an end-on junction with the Glasgow & South Western at Muirkirk, which continued westwards to its main line at Auchinleck and Old Cumnock. The passenger service ceased at the western end in 1951 and from Lanark in 1964. The viaduct is over the infant River Clyde, although there is plenty of space for it to burst its banks in times of flood. *3183*

Below Stonehouse (closed 1965), Strathclyde; DMU from Coalburn, 20 May 1964.

At the end Coalburn had a train northwards in the morning, having come empty stock, and back in the evening, again returning as empty stock! So Alan and I arranged to return on it with special permits and here we are. The station is clean but nearly dead and silent. *3172*

Above Bannockburn, Central; Class 24 No D5125, 3.30pm Aberdeen-Carstairs TPO, 25 May 1968.

These vans, of LMS origin so I am told, used to be detached from the Aberdeen-Glasgow at Stirling, then proceeded under their own power to the West Coast Main Line and London. The skyline is marked by the mountains to the north. C10470

Below Oakley, Central; Class 26 to Stirling, 20 May 1964.

I believe that the freight line from Dunfermline to Kincardine Power Station may be extended, rejoining this former line at Alloa, which would be restored. When I chartered the General Manager's saloons this way from Townend Upper Junction at Dunfermline to Stirling in 1979 I was told that the signalmen might prefer to watch football and not turn up. Because of certain left-wing attitudes hereabouts the train was apparently not shown in the Special Traffic Notice for what it was! We made the journey without incident and at some speed, even pausing at Alloa for photographs. C10421

Below Crail (closed 1965), Fife; DMU, Dundee-Edinburgh, 26 June 1965.

The blind reads incorrectly so that folk at Dundee don't get taken the long way round to Edinburgh unless they so desire – much like the Harrogate route from York to Leeds today. When the through line was shut a branch at the eastern end to St Andrews survived for another five years. *C10334*

Bottom Largo (closed 1965), Fife; DMU, 2.42pm Dundee (Tay Bridge)-Edinburgh (Waverley), 26 June 1965.

My first journey from Edinburgh to Dundee was round the Fife coast, and I always remember it with pleasure. It was another set of coaches like those I rode in from Builth Road (High Level) to Craven Arms, and the steam engine just pottered along, arriving in time for lunch. The sea was nearly always on the horizon. *C10320*

Right Harelaw, Fife; DMU, Dundee-Tayport, 29 August 1965.

This service became redundant as soon as the road bridge opened across the Tay. It was a delightful little branch with charming stations. The track originally formed a horseshoe and rejoined the main line at Leuchars. *C10377*

Below right Elliot Junction (closed 1967), Tayside; Class 40, Edinburgh-Aberdeen, 26 May 1966.

This was the junction for Carmyllie. Whereas the passenger service ceased as long ago as 1929, the goods hung on until 1965, mainly in the form of wagons of seed potatoes; the service could therefore be intermittent. Alan and I hoped to ride it on 19 May 1964 and stayed at Montrose overnight for the purpose. We had brake-van permits, and also on the same day for the freight from Forfar to Careston and from Brechin to Edzell with return to Montrose. We were advised to be in the first coach from Montrose on arrival at Arbroath where a porter would be so sited to tell us to alight if the Carmyllie goods was running or to stay on board and continue to Perth and thus to Forfar if not. In the event there were no seed potatoes to collect. On the express from Perth we were offered mince for lunch, the only time I recall this being on the menu. *C10547*

Above **Lunan Bay, Tayside; Class 40, Edinburgh-Aberdeen, 26 May 1966.**
The train is climbing out of the valley of the Lunan Water near Inverkeilor and hugs the cliffs above the North Sea before turning north and dropping to the River South Esk at Montrose. *C10552*

Below **Usan Junction, Tayside; Class 40, up vans, 26 May 1966.**
The East Coast Main Line is double-track from London to Aberdeen except for a couple of miles near Montrose, presumably to avoid the expense of building wider bridges there. Although the Edinburgh/London service is now augmented here by trains to Glasgow, since closure of the Caledonian main line through Strathmore, I have not heard of the sort of congestion that causes complications at Welwyn North, with demands for a new viaduct and tunnels. *C10559*

Glamis (closed 1956), Tayside; Class 24, Perth-Aberdeen, 18 May 1964.
You can see here what a fine straight main line the Caledonian built through the vale. Again this is a Royal station that has been closed. The late Queen Mother was born nearby. C10609

Left **Carmont, Grampian; Class 47, 5.30pm Aberdeen-Edinburgh, 27 May 1966.**
The main road climbs south out of Stonehaven, but to ease the gradient the railway goes west along the valley of the Carron Water before turning to rejoin it. This is a nice quiet area to watch the trains go by. There used to be a signal box and level crossing at Carmont, but I suspect it will have been modernised. *C10677*

Below left **Stonehaven, Grampian; Class 21, Perth-Aberdeen, 28 May 1966.**
This must be one of the smallest places to have a regular service to London, over 500 miles away. On this occasion the local has been augmented by a van and two vehicles advertising carpets. It will stay near the coast for the rest of its journey, which is sometimes obscured by sea-fret. *C10689*

Above right **Crathes (closed 1966), Grampian; DMU, Aberdeen-Ballater, 16 May 1964.**
Here we are on the Ballater branch again. My diary records that rail chairs on the track here bore the dates 1874 and 1918. The previous night we had brought the car to Perth by Motorail, then joined a train to and from Comrie before travelling north. We cannot go further up the Deeside branch on this train lest we miss the return run in the loop at Banchory and lose the 5.15pm express back from Aberdeen to Perth. We stayed overnight at Bridge of Earn. *C10693*

Below **Huntly, Grampian; DMU, Inverness-Aberdeen, 13 April 1968.**
It is Easter Saturday. A group of us have hired a Morris 1100, HRG 570E, in Aberdeen and will spend the day photographing trains in the Buchan area, as will be obvious from the pictures that follow. Our second stop is here at a location that has changed due to the construction of the town's bypass. You can see the station in the distance. It now has a passing loop on a single line with a yard that sometimes dispatches wagons of timber. *C10728*

Gartly, Grampian; Class 26, Aberdeen-Inverness, 13 April 1968.
The railway here is now a single track and the signals guarding Gartly station (closed within three weeks of our visit) have gone, but the scene is just as beautiful, although the lighting is not always like this, and doubtless there will be more undergrowth. C10723

Grange (closed 1968), Grampian; DMU to Aberdeen, 13 April 1968.
The surviving single line – via Mulben – first comes through here. I think this train originated at Keith. Even now there are two weekday trains from there to Aberdeen within a quarter-hour at 9.32 (SX) and 9.46. C10745

Cairnie Junction (closed 1968), Grampian; DMU shunting, 13 April 1968.
The timetable used to describe this as an exchange platform, and waiting there on a rainy windswept night must have been dreadful. Trains between Aberdeen and Inverness then went either 'via the coast', 'via Mulben' or 'via Dufftown', and boards on the sides of the coaches told you in steam days which was which in the darkness that pervaded the eastern terminus. Dr Beeching would not allow three 'parallel' routes to survive. The train would be split up here by staff uncoupling the coaches, sometimes with the help of lanterns on winter nights. C10734

Above **Grange North Junction, Grampian; DMU to Elgin via the coast, 13 April 1968.**
This route round the coast through Cullen and Buckie has gone, so here are two pictures to remember it by. In the first, also showing our hire car, is the signal box just round the corner from Cairnie Junction, which also controlled a direct chord to the main line towards Keith. *C10736*

Below **Spey Bay (closed 1968), Grampian; Class 26 Elgin-Aberdeen, 13 April 1968.**
In the background of this picture is the enormous viaduct carrying the track above the River Spey near its exit to the sea. Today this has been retained as a public footpath and I took myself to the viaduct last year from the other side. It is well worth a visit. *C10743*

Near Dufftown, Grampian; DMU, Elgin-Aberdeen, 10 July 1961.
You can still obtain this picture on the days that the preservation society here runs its trains to Keith, and there is even a layby on the main road in which to park. A visit to the nearby distillery might pass the time agreeably, too. I had brought the car by Motorail to Perth yet again two days before this picture was taken, and we spent two nights nearby at Rothes in order to explore the Spey Valley line, which diverged at Craigellachie and ran westwards. *2486*

Below Kinloss (closed 1965), Grampian; DMU, Inverness-Aberdeen, 24 August 1965.
Rather a dull day, and just a record shot of a station that had recently shut. C10798

Bottom Forres, Grampian; DMU, Aberdeen-Inverness, 26 August 1965.
The train is crossing over the chord line that connected with the then

– and original – main line from Inverness to Aviemore, which lost its passenger service via Grantown on Spey less than two months later. Without the line south the station layout looks distinctly odd. C10803

Right Kingswood Tunnel, Tayside; two Class 24s, Inverness-Glasgow (Buchanan Street), 22 July 1961.
And so to the Highland main line. My colour picture here is a failure, hence the recourse to Alan's print. What a narrow bore it looks! The train has been passing through woods high above the main road, which it passed above at the other end of the tunnel, since leaving Dunkeld, and now it turns eastwards to Murthly before picking up the general route south. AL1068

Below right Slochd Viaduct, Highland; two Class 24s, Inverness-Glasgow (Buchanan Street), 9 July 1961.
This is now easier of access by car than it was at the time. Last year I went there to see the Safeway train come south, and there was no problem except that the train driver had seen me at Moy and guessed what I had in mind to do – the freight really swung round the corner! Do notice the TPO at the front of the train. AL1448

Left Tomatin Viaduct, Highland; Class 24, Glasgow (Buchanan Street)-Inverness, 11 July 1961.

At the time I recall we were sorry not to see steam. Now the train itself looks its age. We are moving on from Rothes to Kincraig. *AL1449*

Below left Inverness, Milburn Junction, Highland; two Class 24s, Inverness-Glasgow (Buchanan Street), 24 August 1965.

The gantry makes provision for the direct curve between the lines south and north of the River Ness. I joined Motorail here several times and recall the occasion when open wagons were used on the service to Olympia. I was invited to drive the car along the line of trucks to near the front, when there was an almighty crash and the exhaust system became detached from my Triumph 1300. Oh, you're the third one today, cried the attendant excitedly. When I remonstrated with him, he rejoined that I would be given a new system in London, so why worry? *C10911*

Above right Plockton, Highland; Class 26, Inverness-Kyle of Lochalsh, 20 July 1961.

There are two pictures here, taken within a short space of time. Going west is the morning train from Inverness, with the 'Devon Belle' observation saloon at the rear. This originally ran between Waterloo and the West Country and could be turned on the turntable then existing at the Kyle. Loch Carron is at the back of the scene. A leaflet advertising the observation car (although on the Oban line at the time) is reproduced overleaf. *AL1065*

Below Plockton, Highland; Class 26 No D5345, Kyle-Inverness vans, 20 July 1961.

This train has passed through a narrow defile in the mountains and over a substantial embankment. There seems no shortage of traffic. Our holiday in Scotland continues. *AL1353*

Near Diurinish, Highland; Class 26 No D5341, Kyle of Lochalsh-Inverness, 25 August 1965.

As Loch Carron empties into the sea we visit this glorious location looking down from a rocky promontory. The observation saloon can be clearly seen at the back of the train. We are now at the back of the book and I hope you have enjoyed the journey as much as those travelling from the Kyle on that summer evening nearly 40 years ago at the dawn of the diesels. *C11056*

INDEX